# GUIDE TO THE THYSSEN BORNEMISZA MUSEUM

SECOND EDITION
REVISED BY
TOMÀS LLORENS

TOMÀS LLORENS
MARÍA DEL MAR BOROBIA
CONCHA VELA

"An artist's talent is a gift to the whole world. When I began my collection, the main asset I possessed was my eyes, which are a gift from God. Painters do not make their works for the eyes of only one man. My bequest as a collector is to share my paintings, and I can only repay God's gift by making it possible for more than one man to see and understand the talent of the artist".

*Baron Hans Heinrich Thyssen-Bornemisza de Kaszon, 1983*

Production and printing: LUNWERG EDITORES S.A.
Beethoven, 12 - 08021 Barcelona. Tel.: 93 201 59 33. Fax: 93 201 15 87
Sagasta, 27 - 28036 Madrid. Tel.: 91 593 00 58. Fax: 91 593 00 70

I.S.B.N.: 84-88474-48-2
Depósito Legal: B-38634-1998

Layout design: Daniel Gil
Cover design: Sonia Sánchez/Pep Carrió

PRINTED IN SPAIN

# Index

# SECOND FLOOR

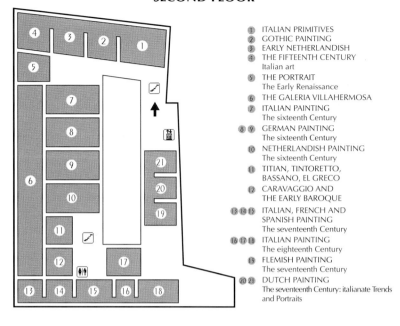

# FIRST FLOOR

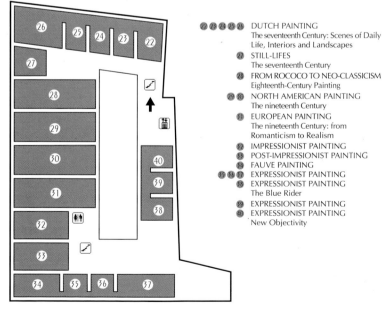

# GROUND FLOOR

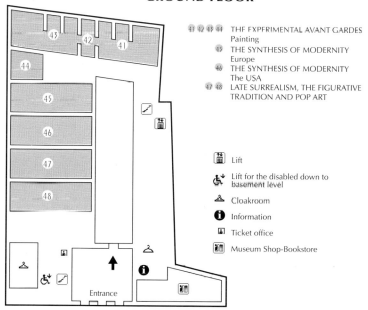

**41 42 43 44** THE EXPERIMENTAL AVANT GARDES
Painting
**45** THE SYNTHESIS OF MODERNITY
Europe
**46** THE SYNTHESIS OF MODERNITY
The USA
**47 48** LATE SURREALISM, THE FIGURATIVE
TRADITION AND POP ART

Lift

Lift for the disabled down to
basement level

Cloakroom

Information

Ticket office

Museum Shop-Bookstore

Entrance

# BASEMENT LEVEL

Auditorium

Access for
Museum personnel only

Area for
temporary exhibitions

Stairs

Restroom

Lift for the disabled up to
ground floor

Telephones

Cafeteria-Restaurant

## Introduction

The works of art on display in this museum were collected by the Thyssen-Bornemisza family over two generations. The collection was started in the second decade of the present century by Baron Heinrich Thyssen-Bornemisza, and considerably enlarged by his son Hans Heinrich, the present Baron.

In 1988 the Spanish government and the Thyssen-Bornemisza family reached an agreement whereby the collection, consisting of 775 paintings, would be on display to the Spanish public for a period of nine and a half years. Following the restoration of the Palacio de Villahermosa, chosen as the site of the new museum, the Museo Thyssen-Bornemisza opened its doors to the public on 10 October 1992. A few months later, on 21 June 1993, the loan arrangement was superseded by the permanent acquisition of the collection by the Spanish State.

While a selection of around 60 paintings from the collection are displayed at the Pedralbes Monastery in Barcelona, the remainder of the collection, 715 paintings, are permanently on view in the Palacio de Villahermosa, Madrid.

The Palacio de Villahermosa was built in the last years of the eighteenth century and the early years of the nineteenth century and is a fine example of the Madrid Neo-Classical architectural style. The architect Rafael Moneo has adapted the building to its present function, creating a new interior layout and room sequence. The galleries are arranged around a central area and are of varying dimensions, of which the largest is axially aligned with the building's facade on the Paseo del Prado. The resulting interior has successfully harmonised a modern architectural approach with the building's original function as a palace, and with the traditional layout of the classical museum and art gallery.

Located on the basement level are the museum's temporary exhibition rooms, the cafeteria and the conference hall. In addition to the central atrium, the ground floor houses the entrance hall, bookshop and cloakroom. The rest of this floor, and the two upper floors, are given over to the display of the permanent collection.

The collection has been displayed following a chronological and historical sequence. The oldest paintings have been hung on the top floor as this has lower ceilings and the paintings can be lit by natural overhead light. Any visitor wishing to view the collection in chronological order should therefore cross the central atrium on the ground floor, and take the lift or stairs to the top floor. The room numbers indicate the sequence in which they should be viewed, moving in a right-hand direction around the central atrium and proceeding down from floor to floor as the visit progresses.

The galleries have been hung with the intention of creating a stylistic unity: each one of them corresponds with what might be described as a chapter in the history of art.

NOTE: In the pages that follow, the first mention of any artist includes the dates of his or her birth and death in brackets after the name. In some cases the titles of the paintings as they are given in the text are in an abbreviated form. At the end of the guide each work is listed with its full title, date (when known), medium, dimensions (in centimetres, height before width) and catalogue number.

# SECOND FLOOR

# 1 Italian Primitives

Our ideas about the Italian artists of the fourteenth and fifteenth centuries (traditionally known as the "Italian Primitives") are still moulded by the writings of Giorgio Vasari (1511-1574), the Florentine painter, architect and writer considered to be the first art historian. To Vasari we owe the idea that the work of these artists represented a process of progress and regeneration of the arts.

Following ideas to be found in Aristotle's *Poetics,* Vasari proposed that the aim of artistic creation was to imitate nature, and his notion of the history of art is very much based on this criterion. For Vasari, painting reached its first qualitative peak in Antiquity, only to fall away in the Middle Ages, when artists were unable to represent nature adequately: a failure evident to Vasari in the Byzantine art which he saw in Italy. It would fall to Tuscan artists, in particular Giotto, to break free of the Byzantine influence and embark on the path back to naturalistic representation in a continuing process which culminated in the early sixteenth century in the art of Michelangelo, which equalled and even surpassed the art of Antiquity.

While Vasari's notions may be far from our own today, they allow us some perception of the internal development underlying the panorama of Italian art of the fourteenth and fifteenth centuries: it was an ongoing process of achievement, in short a "re-birth", realised through a process which based itself on the dichotomy between the old, "decadent" style of painting, and the new, "regenerated" mode.

The visitor can appreciate the contrast between the old and new styles by comparing *The Virgin and Child* (cat. 256) by the Master of the Magdalen (active in the second half of the thirteenth century) with the *Christ and the Woman of Samaria at the Well* (cat. 133) by Duccio di Buoninsegna (active around 1278-1319). Less than twenty years separates the production of these two works, both painted in Tuscany around 1300, but they reflect two completely different approaches to painting. In the first painting, the artist presents the holy figures frontally on a flat background. In the second, the idea is to present a story (which the spectator would have heard or read in the Gospels) and with this aim in mind the painter arranges the figures within a sort of stage set which has a sense of receding space. The first style, the so-called "Byzantine" only requires the artist to be able to paint a limited repertoire of figures, lines, forms and colours, as any craftsman could do. The

**133. Duccio di Buoninsegna**
*Christ and the Woman of Samaria at the Well, 1310-11*

Tempera on panel. 43.5 x 46 cm

rather narrow conventions of this style leave little room for innovation. The second mode of painting, however, demands that the artist be continually seeking new motifs (human figures, gestures, facial expressions, buildings, everyday objects, drapery etc.) drawn from his observation of the world around him to make the narrative of the painting lifelike. The requirements for success in the first mode of painting were already set down for the artist: in the second he was obliged to seek them out in a continuing process of observation.

Even though the picture might be composed of a wide variety of different elements, it needs to have a coherent overall structure, hence the development of the idea of *composition*, which might be

# Italian
# Primitives

defined as the skill or art of subordinating each individual element of the picture to the overall aim or effect desired by the artist.

The imitation of nature, an ability to express emotions through telling a story, the depiction of spatial recession, and compositional structure were the new criteria which guided the development of Italian painting from the early years of the fourteenth century.

Within the work of the leading Tuscan artists of this period it has been traditional to contrast that of the Florentine artists with their Sienese counterparts. The first group, represented by Giotto and his pupils, understood composition as the balance and counter-balance of bodies, masses, volumes and gestures, evident, for example, in the *Crucifixion* (cat. 151) by Agnolo Gaddi (active around 1369-1396).

With regard to the Sienese school, whose principal artists, along with Duccio, were Simone Martini (1284-1344), Pietro Lorenzetti and Ugolino de Nerio (documented between 1317-1327), the idea of composition was primarily that of harmonising the linear design, characterised by fluid and stylised lines, with the colour, characterised by densely saturated tones. One artist of the Sienese school, Giovanni di Paolo (circa 1399-1482), whose work is characterised by a unique, highly personal style, achieved a synthesis of the Florentine and late Gothic styles. His panel painting, *Saint Catherine before the Pope in Avignon* (cat. 162), depicts a scene in which the treatment of spatial perspective and the conception of the figures already shows an assimilation of the new approach, despite the use of the traditional gold for the cloth in the background.

While the Florentine manner was to win out ultimately, mainly due to the development of the use of perspective in the fifteenth century, Sienese art had the greater influence in the short term.

This influence extended to other parts of Italy, as we can see in the *Crucifixion* (cat. 425) by Vitale da Bologna (circa 1300-1359/61). With its inclination towards narrative fantasy and an emphasis on emotions, the Sienese style was a major factor in the development of the so-called International Gothic art of the last quarter of the fourteenth century.

425. **Vitale da Bologna**
*The Crucifixion, c.1335*

Tempera on panel. 93 x 51.2 cm

17

# 2 Gothic Painting

International Gothic, a distinct and homogenous style which combined Italian, particularly Sienese characteristics with regionally varying elements, spread across the whole of Europe in the late fourteenth century. Its existence was threatened by the dawnings of the early Renaissance in the first third of the fifteenth century. But the growth of the Renaissance, which began in a few Italian and Netherlandish cities, was slow to extend itself and had to wait until the sixteenth century (in some countries until the end of that century) before it penetrated the whole of Europe, definitively eclipsing the International Gothic style.

The earliest pictures in this room date from the middle of the fourteenth century, a period in which the Gothic style was not yet a uniform and completely accepted manner of painting. This explains the highly individual style of the *Triptych of the Holy Face of Christ* (cat. 44), by the Master Bertram (circa 1330/40-1414) who worked in the area around Hamburg.

During the course of the fifteenth century, at a time when the wealth of many cities considerably increased, there was an ever increasing demand for works of art to fulfil religious requirements. As a consequence the Gothic style increasingly divided into different regional and local schools. A late example of this phenomenon is the group of eight panels on show in this room on the subject of the Four Evangelists (cat. 233 to 240) which date from the last third of the fifteenth century. They were painted by the Munich-based artist Gabriel Mälesskircher (circa 1430/40-1495) who trained Michael Wolgemut, in his turn the teacher of Dürer.

Among the paintings on show in this room, the most typical and also finest example of the late Gothic style is *The Assumption of the Virgin* (cat. 210) by Johann Koerbecke (circa 1420-1490). Painted just before 1457, the panel comes from an altarpiece in the Cistercian monastery of Marienfeld. The artist worked in the area around Münster, a city which, just two generations later, would witness one of the most notable and bloody episodes of the Reformation. The painting's emotional intensity, its elegant faces and gestures, the sumptuous colours of the draperies, its flamelike composition and the sinuousness of the lines are all precursors of the artistic taste and cultural climate which Huizinga was to call the Autumn of the Middle Ages.

210. **Johann Koerbecke**
*The Assumption of the Virgin, before 1457*

Oil on panel. 93.1 x 64.2 cm

# 3 Early Netherlandish Painting

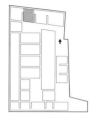

The artistic Renaissance which took place in the Low Countries was founded on a similar cultural and social climate to that of its Italian counterpart. Its principal artistic aim was also the same: that of the imitation of nature. However these two very similar movements differed in the way they applied this principle. By nature abstract and methodical, the painting of the early Italian Renaissance focused on the control of spatial organisation and culminated in the conquest of rational perspective. The art of the Netherlandish Renaissance, tactile and instinctive, was centred on a fascination with the distinctive qualities of objects.

The rational nature of the Italian Renaissance meant that it developed in a relatively uniform and focused way. The artistic development in the Low Countries took a much less direct path and one which was dictated by the great painters of that time. Thus, the further away from their art we move, the closer we find ourselves to Gothic art once more.

The first of these great masters was Jan van Eyck (circa 1390-1441), the legendary founder of Netherlandish painting. The subject of the Thyssen-Bornemisza diptych is *The Annunciation* (cat. 137). Rather than presenting the angel, the Virgin and the Holy Spirit directly, the artist opted to depict them through painted sculptural versions. Elegantly arranged and proportioned, finely modelled, imbued with a super-human beauty, the figures act in relation to each other without forming a real group. They seem as if sculpted in high relief from a stone which, under the light, gives off the tone of old silver, reflected against a background of a shiny black stone. So accurate is Van Eyck's representation that we can tell what type of limestone he was painting.

Other religious paintings hang in the same room as this great masterpiece. Together they form an exceptional grouping, both in terms of quality and comprehensiveness. Two of the most important should be mentioned: by Jacques Daret (active between 1418 and 1468) and Roger van der Weyden (circa 1399-1464), both pupils of Robert Campin (an artist whose work can be seen in room 5). Daret's painting is a beautiful *Adoration of the Christ Child* (cat. 124), from a group of paintings executed for the Abbey of Saint Vaast in Arras, the only known work by the artist. His contemporary, Roger van der Weyden, is represented here by a *Virgin Enthroned* (cat. 435), whose tiny scale is matched by its monumental conception. Also of small dimensions is another masterpiece from the collection, *The Virgin of the dry Tree* (cat. 121) by Petrus Christus (circa 1410-1472/73). The painting's subject matter is a Christological metaphor based on the Old Testament. The Virgin, bearer of the Messiah, is like a flowering branch with which God brought to life again the dry tree of the chosen people. Hanging from the branches are fifteen letter "A"s in gold, symbolising so many Hail Marys. This small picture could be used for saying prayers in the manner of a miniature rosary.

Four more works of outstanding quality date from the last third of the fifteenth century. The severe and heartfelt *Lamentation* (cat. 142) by Juan de Flandes (active between 1496 and 1519) was painted in Spain. A triptych on the same subject (cat. 252) by the Master of the Legend of Saint Lucy (active around 1475-around 1501) combines a tragic eloquence which the artist had learned from Van der Weyden, with a gen-

137. a and b. **Jan van Eyck**
*The Annunciation Diptych, c.1435-41*

Panel. Each wing 39 x 24 cm

# Early Netherlandish Painting

tler Italianate feeling which was prevalent in Bruges in the last decades of the century. In contrast to this painting, the *Crucifixion* (cat. 269) by the Master of the Virgo inter Virgines (active between 1480 and 1495), is a remarkable witness to the survival of the Gothic style on the periphery of the Low Countries, with its crowded composition, exaggerated colouring and narrative density. Another work which looks back rather than forward, albeit in a different way, is the equally magnificent *Calvary* (cat. 125) by Gerard David (circa 1460-1523). In it the artist, who was both the most Italianate and also the last of the great masters of the golden age of painting in Bruges, deliberately looks back in order to evoke the marvellous works of Van Eyck, Campin and Van der Weyden.

124. **Jacques Daret**
*The Adoration of the Christ Child, 1434-35*

Oil on panel. 59.5 x 53 cm

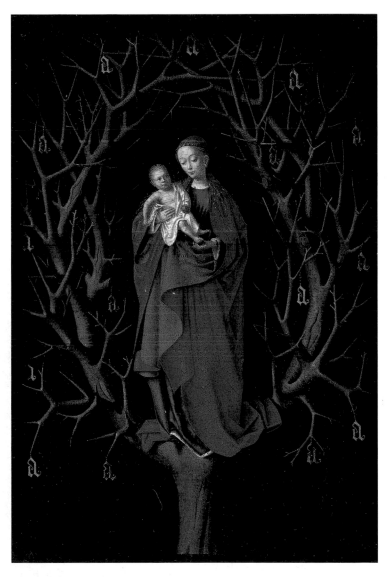

121. **Petrus Christus**
*The Virgin of the dry Tree, c.1450*

Oil on panel. 17.4 x 12.3 cm

# 4 15th-century Italian Painting

The oldest painting on display in this room is a *Crucifixion* by an anonymous Neapolitan artist (cat. 94). The tragic intensity of the expressions, the dense colouring and the fluid treatment of the brushwork all suggest considerable Flemish influence, while the solid placement of the figures within the spatial setting and the precise manner in which the city and its surrounding hills recede into the background are obviously Italian. This painting was previously attributed to Colantonio, the teacher of Antonello da Messina, but specialists now think it is the work of a French or Netherlandish painter whose identity has still to be established but who must have worked in Naples during the reign of Alfonso V the Magnanimous.

The room contains a notable group of painting from Ferrara, a city whose ducal court was the focus of a significant literary and artistic culture in the late fifteenth and early sixteenth centuries. One of the best Ferrarese artists is Ercole de' Roberti (circa 1450-1496), represented here by a scene from the voyage of the Argonauts as told by Ovid (cat. 344). Only the refined ambience of a humanist court could have produced this representation of a mythological subject at such an early date.

The work of the Ferrarese artists, together with artists from the Venetian mainland (such as Marco Zoppo, 1433-1478, and Alvise Vivarini, circa 1445-circa 1505) lead us on to the magnificent display of early sixteenth-century Venetian painting which can be seen in room 7. However, the most important painting in the room points towards other artistic directions. Probably painted around the last decade of the fifteenth century, the *Risen Christ* (cat. 61) exhibits the synthesis of perspective, drawing, volume and colour which Dürer admired in the work of Giovanni Bellini at that date. However, the *Risen Christ*, at once majestically super-human yet tangibly real, has little of the Venetian about it. The painting was formerly attributed to Bramante but it is now thought more likely to be a work by his pupil known as El Bramantino (circa 1465-1530). By comparing this painting with the Neapolitan Crucifixion described above, it is possible to see just how much progress had been made since Italian and Netherlandish painting first converged four decades earlier. We are now on the threshold of the High Renaissance.

61. **Bramantino**
*The Risen Christ*

Oil on panel. 109 x 73 cm

# 5 The Portrait in the Early Renaissance

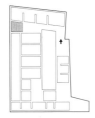

The development of the portrait and the dawning of the Renaissance are closely connected. The main purpose of Medieval painting was the depiction of people and events from the Bible and other holy or devotional texts. Artists sought to represent what could not otherwise be seen in normal life. The idea of painting representing daily reality rather than supernatural or miraculous events involved an enormous cultural shift.

Furthermore, the fact that the portrait was the first secular theme to be developed by Renaissance artists and also the most important, gives some idea of the change in values which the Renaissance heralded. It was precisely this change that prompted Jacob Burckhardt to make the role of the individual one of the central themes of his famous study published in 1860, *The Civilisation of the Renaissance in Italy.*

This does not mean that the portrait did not also have a variety of practical functions. For a long time it was associated with religious painting: the donor who commissioned and paid for an altarpiece would be painted as a spectator or participant in the super-natural scene represented. Alongside the religious sentiments of the donor it is easy to understand the desire to have one's appearance recorded for one's contemporaries and also for posterity. Having got this far, the fact that painting could achieve an accurate visual record of physical appearance and character began to be exploited for other ends, for example betrothal or wedding portraits. Marriages at this date were often contracted for political and economic reasons, without the couple to be married ever having met or even seen each other. In these circumstances the family or intermediaries involved in the match turned to artists in order to help dispel the understandable anxieties of the betrothed couple. At the end of the fifteenth century this practice developed in some European countries into the idea of the double portrait, painted to commemorate the marriage. Another practice, as happened in Venice, was for a patron to simply commission his own portrait, or that of another person.

The interrelationship between character and physical appearance, between the spiritual and physical aspects of beauty, is the subject of the Latin epigram by the poet Martial which is inscribed on the portrait of Giovanna Tornabuoni (cat. 158) painted in 1488 by the Florentine artist Domenico Ghirlandaio (1449-1494). The epigram runs, "If the artist could have painted here the character

ARS VTINAM MORES
ANIMVM QVE EFFINGERE
POSSES PVLCHRIOR IN TER
RIS NVLLA TABELLA FORET
·MCCCCLXXXVIII·

158. **Domenico Ghirlandaio**
*Portrait of Giovanna Tornabuoni, 1488*

Panel. 77 x 49 cm

# The Portrait in the
# Early Renaissance

and moral virtues, there would be no finer painting on earth".

There is probably a degree of social convention as well as political expediency involved here (the marriage of Giovanna degli Albizzi with a member of the Tornabuoni family, allies of the Medici, resulted in a period of peace for Florence), but the elegant Latin motto also affirms an important belief: for Renaissance man there was a profound relationship between physical and spiritual perfection. This belief explains the enormous importance which art attained during the Renaissance: by capturing physical beauty through painting, as though looking in a mirror, it should also be possible to capture the subject's spiritual beauty in the same way.

The *Portrait of Giovanna Tornabuoni* is hung here together with twelve other early Renaissance portraits: five Netherlandish and five Italian, one German and one Hispano-Flemish.

Of these, the oldest Netherlandish and the oldest Italian should not perhaps be considered true portraits. *A Monk with a Cross* (cat. 130) by Domenico Veneziano (1400/10-1461) from the 1440s depicts, according to one plausible suggestion, San Filippo Benizzi, head of the Servite Order who died at the end of the thirteenth century. It is most unlikely that the artist would have known what the sitter really looked like. The opposite was probably the case with the *Posthumous Portrait of Wenceslas, Duke of Brabant* (cat. 11), painted around 1405, even though the Duke had died in 1383. His features were probably known to the artist through other paintings, sculptures or drawings. The comparison between this very early Netherlandish painting and Domenico Veneziano's panel, executed almost four decades later, shows us just how much more advanced the art of portraiture was in the Low Countries than in Italy in the first half of the fifteenth century.

Nothing demonstrates the initial superiority of Flemish portraiture better than the *Portrait of Robert de Masmines* (cat. 74) by Robert Campin (circa 1375-1444), painted just before 1430. Painted a few years before Van Eyck's Annunciation diptych (see room 3), Campin has modelled the head of the Burgundian soldier with all the precision of a maker of scientific instruments.

There is no portrait in Italy which would not pale beside Campin's masterpiece until we arrive at the late works by Antonello da Messina (circa 1430-1479), painted during his time in Venice in the 1470s. While his *Portrait of a Man* (cat. 18) may not attain the exactitude of Campin's panel, it surpasses it in its realisation of

**74. Robert Campin**
*Portrait of a thick-set Man
(Robert de Masmines?), c.1425(?)*

Oil on panel. 34.5 x 23.7 cm

**18. Antonello da Messina**
*Portrait of a Man, c.1475-76*

Oil on panel. 27.5 x 21 cm

**284a. Hans Memling**
*Portrait of a Young Man praying, c.1485*

Oil on panel. 29.2 x 22.5 cm

**141. Juan de Flandes**
*Portrait of an Infanta
(Catherine of Aragon?), c. 1496*

Oil on panel. 31.5 x 22 cm

29

# The Portrait in the Early Renaissance

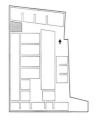

volume, in the liveliness of expression, and in the magisterial treatment of light. Times had changed since Campin, painting techniques had become more sophisticated, as had the tastes of art lovers and collectors. Another portrait with a marvellous handling of light is the *Portrait of a Young Man praying* (cat. 284) painted by an artist of Antonello's generation, Hans Memling (circa 1435-1494), in Bruges in the last third of the fifteenth century. The painting is bathed in a more delicate light than Antonello's panel and is even more precise in colouring, although perhaps less so in its modelling of volume and form.

Chronologically the group concludes with portraits of members of the reigning houses of Castille and England. Stylistically they are backward-looking, being painted well into the sixteenth century by which time this small-scale format had been superseded by the formal Italian type (see room 7). Both revive the great Flemish portrait type of the preceding century, filtered in the case of the *Infanta de Castille* by Juan de Flandes (cat. 141) by a gentle melancholy and a highly individual palette, and in the case of *King Henry VIII* (cat. 191) by Hans Holbein (1497/8-1543) by the desire to express the courtly splendour of a monarch who was learned, young, powerful and rich. Painted at a time when the painters of Florence, Rome and Venice were opening up new artistic horizons, these two portraits conclude one of the most fascinating chapters in the history of painting.

**191. Hans Holbein the Younger**
*Portrait of Henry VIII of England, c. 1534-36*

Oil on panel. 28 x 20 cm

# 6 The Galería Villahermosa

This space is unique within the architectural layout of the Palacio de Villahermosa. It is not so much a room as what would be called in Italian a *galleria*: a long corridor situated parallel to one of the building's facades, often on the top floor and lit by a sequence of windows or balconies. Partly due to the excellent lighting which such spaces enjoyed, they were often used as a type of art gallery where collectors of the Italian Renaissance displayed their paintings and sculptures.

In the case of the present space, designed by the architect Rafael Moneo to run the length of the facade on the Paseo del Prado, the Galería opens onto six rooms which are lit from above (in this guide numbered as rooms 7 to 13). These rooms display sixteenth-century paintings divided into three different schools: one room devoted to Italian paintings of the first half of the sixteenth century; two rooms of German paintings; one of Flemish paintings and another two of Italian paintings of the second half of the sixteenth century.

By calling this gallery the Galería Villahermosa the Museo Thyssen-Bornemisza has aimed to preserve the memory of the Dukes of Villahermosa, the builders and first occupiers of the building which bore their name for two centuries and which now houses the Museo Thyssen-Bornemisza following its extensive remodelling.

The paintings hung here have been chosen to recall the type of art which would originally have been hung in a gallery of this sort in the sixteenth century. On view are a selection of sixteenth-century portraits, mainly Italian, but also German and Netherlandish, arranged (as would have been the case in the sixteenth century) more for their decorative impact than by any historical or chronological criteria.

The large number of portraits displayed in this gallery and in the surrounding rooms is one of the distinguishing features of the museum's collection, in that the first Baron Thyssen-Bornesmiza preferred portraiture to any other genre of painting.

330. **Raphael**
*Portrait of a young Man (Alessandro de' Medici?), c.1515*

Oll on panel. 44 x 29,4 cm

# 7 16th-century Italian Painting

No other period of art has been so influential as the High Renaissance. While its principal centre was Rome, so important was the role of Florentine artists, humanists and patrons that it could fairly be said that its origins lay in Florence. The artistic formulae of the High Renaissance spread from Italy to the rest of Europe, becoming the established canon for the teaching of painting, sculpture and architecture.

In sixteenth-century Italy, Rome was not the only major centre. Venetian art, which saw a great flowering that lasted for seventy-five years, exercised an enormous if intermittent influence on later art, equal to that of Rome, particularly in painting.

In addition to Roman classicism and the Venetian style, any thorough survey of 16th-century Italian art would be incomplete without a reference to the complex phenomenon of Mannerism, which followed on the High Renaissance in Rome, Florence and other regions of Italy. The rise of Bolognese Classicism in the last quarter of the century was also important.

The paintings on show in this room together indicate something of the richness of Italian art in the sixteenth century.

One of the most celebrated paintings in this collection is the *Young Knight in a Landscape* (cat. 82) by the Venetian artist Vittore Carpaccio (c.1460/65-1525/26). The painting is usually considered to be a portrait but the sitter's identity is unknown. The exact significance of the animals, plants and allegorical figures within the landscape have also yet to be explained, although it is possible that they may relate to a particular public or military situation or event of the time. It certainly seems plausible that the artist and the patron set out to represent the subject of the painting as a young Christian knight endowed with the qualities and virtues commonly described in the courtly romances of the period. The painting is one of Carpaccio's masterpieces. Painted in 1510 it relates more closely to painting of the previous century than to the new art of the High Renaissance. This can be seen by comparing it with *The Annunciation* (cat. 38) by Gentile Bellini (1429-1507), painted around 1470, which has been hung in this room as a point of comparison with the work by Carpaccio who was Gentile Bellini's pupil.

Gentile Bellini's school is important for a correct understanding of Venetian painting at the beginning of the sixteenth century, but it came to an end following the death of Carpaccio. Instead, it

**82. Vittore Carpaccio**
*Young Knight in a Landscape, 1510*

Oil on canvas. 218.5 x 151.5 cm

## 16th-century
## Italian Painting

was that of his brother Giovanni (circa 1430-1516) which represented the main current of Venetian art, extending almost to the end of the century. There is some doubt as to the exact date of Giovanni Bellini's *Sacra Conversazione ("Nunc dimittis")* (cat. 39) but it is generally thought to be from the first decade of the sixteenth century. The painting's frontality, its internal organisation and the static nature of the composition as well as the fullness of the forms all suggest the formal values of Roman low-relief sculpture. The painting reflects the introduction of a new classicism into Venetian art by Bellini in 1505 with his altarpiece for the church of San Zaccaria, the artistic starting point for his followers Giorgione (circa 1476/8-1510), Sebastiano del Piombo (circa 1485-1547) and Titian (circa 1488-1576). The Thyssen painting would certainly seem to be a late work by the artist judging from the degree of psychological abstraction of the figures, the gentleness of the landscape and the way in which the forms are almost dissolved in order to achieve more glowing and abstract colours.

Painted in Rome around 1511 or 1512, the *Portrait of Ferry Carondelet* (cat. 369) is one of Sebastiano del Piombo's masterpieces, and a painting still very much influenced by Venetian art. For many years it was believed to be by Raphael. The large format and monumental composition indicate a new type of portraiture which was developed in Rome during the pontificate of Leo X, and one which suggests a more public function for portraiture than that previously enjoyed by the small format portraits of the fifteenth century.

Another pupil of Giovanni Bellini was Palma Vecchio (circa 1480-1528). He used Bellini's compositional invention for his own *Sacra Conversazione* (cat. 309), on show in this room. Palma's version, painted around 1522, six years after the death of his teacher, is more lively in its gestures and movements, and clearly shows the influence of the new style introduced by Titian in his large paintings for the church of Santa Maria Gloriosa. Another work close in style to Titian (it was in fact attributed to him for many years) is the portrait known as *La Bella* (cat. 310), which must have been painted by Palma around 1525. The sitter's identity is not known but it is worth remembering that at this period portraits were sometimes painted and bought for no other reason than the beauty of the sitter: we know, for example, that the French king François I bought portraits for this reason.

**39. Giovanni Bellini**
*Sacra Conversazione, 1505-10*

Oil on panel. 62 x 82.5 cm

**369. Sebastiano del Piombo**
*Portrait of Ferry Carondelet
with his Secretaries, 1510-12*

Oil on panel. 112.5 x 87 cm

**310. Palma Vecchio**
*Portrait of a young Woman
called "La Bella", c.1525*

Oil on canvas. 95 x 80 cm

Chronologically the latest example of Venetian painting on show in this room is another work by Titian, painted in 1555. This is an official portrait of *Doge Francesco Venier* (cat. 405). While the compositional format varies little from the earlier portrait by Sebastiano del Piombo in this room, the style of painting is completely different. Gone are the large planes of colour which characterised Venetian painting of the first two decades of the century. The artist's palette is now reduced and the dark earth tones, the purple and gold are broken down to an infinity of differing tonalities. The paintings on show in room 11 are witnesses to this pictorial revolution.

Aside from Venetian art, which is the most fully represented school in this room, there are two interesting compositions by Piero di Cosimo (1461/62-1527) and Fra Bartolommeo (1472-1517) (cat. 320 and 29) painted in Florence in the early years of the sixteenth century.

Having reached its culmination in the High Renaissance, Italian painting embarked on a profound change of direction, leading to a style which modern art historians have called Mannerism. Three major works on display here give a good idea of its characteristics. *The Virgin and Child with Saint John and Saint Jerome* (cat. 33) by the Sienese artist Domenico Beccafumi (1486-1551) is perhaps the most spectacular: the tight composition, the sinuousness of the lines and above all the colours reflect the feverish spirit of innovation which gripped Italian art in the 1520s. The manipulation of perspective and the mood, at once fervent but restrained, of the *Young Man portrayed as Saint Sebastian* (cat. 64) by Bronzino (1503-1572), or the cold elegance and calculated geometry of the *Portrait of a Lady* (cat. 145) by Pier-Francesco Foschi (1502-1567) are other aspects of the Mannerist style.

**33. Domenico Beccafumi**
*The Virgin and Child with Saint John and Saint Jerome, c. 1523-24*

Oil on panel. 85.5 cm diameter

# 8-9 16th-century German Painting

The Gothic trends which we observed in room 3 are still evident in German painting of the late fifteenth century. Good examples are the works of the anonymous artist working in Düren (cat. 259) and the paintings of the Master of Grossgmain (cat. 250) on show in room 8. This late survival of the Gothic was gradually overlaid by the influence of Netherlandish and Italian art, and a work such as the *Virgin and Child with Saint Margaret and Saint Catherine* (cat. 308) by a follower of Michael Pacher (1430/35-1498) combines a mastery of perspective and an almost Ferrarese elegance in the figures with a traditional Gothic gold background.

The traditional nature of German devotional painting of the early sixteenth century may be due to the fact that the majority of patronage came from the urban bourgeoisie. Although stylistically old fashioned, the painting of this period displayed a high level of skill and enormous visual impact, as in the case of the spectacular *Crucifixion* by Derick Baegert (circa 1440-circa 1515). The painting was dismantled and broken up into smaller panels earlier in its history. The five surviving panels now on show in this room (cat. 22-26) were reunited over many years in the Thyssen-Bornemisza Collection.

Other notable paintings on religious subjects in room 8 are the expressive *Annunciation to Saint Anne* (cat. 380) by Bernhard Strigel (1460-1528) and the *Triptych of the Celestial Rosary* by Hans Kulmbach (circa 1485-1521), a painting in which the artist has attempted to impose a classical composition on a subject which was traditionally treated in an allegorical mode. In the *Adoration of the Christ Child* (cat. 69) by Barthel Bruyn the Elder (1493-1555) Italian stylistic influences meld with a Netherlandish feeling, a combination still more obvious in his portrait of a man and woman (cat. 67 and 68). Another fusion of these two schools is evident in the *Virgin and Child with a Bunch of Grapes* (cat. 114) by Lucas Cranach the Elder (1472-1553). Painted in the first decade of the sixteenth century, the intense colours and expressive treatment of the landscape link this painting to the style of the-called Danube School.

Towering above all these artists is Dürer (1471-1528), the key figure in German Renaissance art. His panel painting *Christ among the Doctors* (cat. 134), dated 1506, was painted in Italy over a period of just five days according to the inscription next to the signature. The variety of figures and the novelty of the composition, combined with the deliberately summary style gives the painting

**114. Lucas Cranach the Elder**

*The Virgin and Child with a Bunch of Grapes, c. 1509-10*

Oil on panel. 71.5 x 44.2 cm

## 16th-century German Painting

rather the feeling of an artistic challenge, as if Dürer, stimulated by the Italian surroundings in which he found himself, had decided to show the best of his own art. Some of the half-length figures clustered around the young Christ seem to be inspired by those in Leonardo's drawings. The young hands of Christ, juxtaposed with the old ones of his principal opponent, create a lively grouping which the artist has placed in the centre of the composition.

The onset of the Reformation and the subsequent conflicts which it generated in German society had a profound effect on the history of painting. One result was that as from the end of the first quarter of the sixteenth century the Church no longer commissioned works of art, as can be seen in room 9.

The paintings of Lucas Cranach the Elder (whose *Virgin and Child with a Bunch of Grapes* hangs in room 8) and those of his sons Hans (circa 1513-1537) and Lucas the Younger (1515-1586), hung together in room 9, form a group which together illustrate the pictorial taste which prevailed during the early years of the Reformation in one of the main princely courts of the Empire, that of the Elector of Saxony. Worth singling out is the *The Nymph of the Spring* (cat. 115). She reclines by a pool which is fed by a stream. The composition, which exists in several autograph versions, has been linked to the idea of the Fountain of Castalia, the inspiration of poets and philosophers, and also with the theme of the sleeping Venus. Cupid's bow and arrows hang idly from a tree trunk. While the theme has strong Neo-platonic overtones redolent of Italian humanism, it would be difficult to imagine a less Italianate treatment of the subject.

Perhaps the most intense treatment of the German sixteenth-century manner is to be found in the work of Hans Baldung called Grien (1484/85-1545), an artist formed alongside Dürer and stylistically close to Cranach. He painted the *Adam and Eve* (cat. 27), choosing to emphasise the sensual aspect of the subject and the theme of Original Sin. Grien also painted the *Portrait of a Lady* (cat. 28), drawing on a female type developed by Cranach. In this unusual portrait, illuminated by a strong light source which brings out the softness of the modelling, the subject's enigmatic expression troubles the spectator. Amazingly, Grien achieves his effects with only a very limited palette of a green, two reds, black and white.

With the disappearance of religious commissions, portraiture became the dominant genre. The richness of the Thyssen Collec-

134. **Albrecht Dürer**
*Christ among the Doctors, 1506*
Oil on panel. 64.3 x 80.3 cm

tion in this area allows for a complete overview of the subject in the sixteenth century, starting from its origins at the end of the previous century.

The artist Michael Wolgemut (1434/37-1519) developed the prototype of the portrait with an imaginary background in his *Portrait of Levinus Memminger* (cat. 440) whose sitter had connections with the city of Nuremberg. Bernhard Strigel's *Portrait of a Man* (cat. 379) is of the same type. Hans Wertinger (circa 1465/70-1533) painted one of the first ever full-length portraits with his *Portrait of the Court Jester 'The Knight Christopher'* (cat. 434) dated 1515.

Other forms of portraiture which can be seen in the Thyssen Collection include the double portrait of *Coloman Helmschmid and Agnes Breu* (cat. 244) by Breu the Elder (circa 1480-1537) and an anonymous artist. The couple are set within semi-circular arches. The famous Munich artist Barthel Beham (1502-1540) painted the husband and wife *Ruprecht Stüf* and *Ursula Rudolph* (cat. 36-

# 16th-century
# German Painting

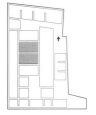

**115. Lucas Cranach the Elder**
*The Nymph of the Spring, 1530-34*

Oil on panel. 75 x 120 cm

37) in over half-length format, making full use of the curtains in the background for artistic effect.

Albrecht Altdorfer (circa 1480-1538), founder of the Danube School, used the three-quarter length format at a relatively early date in his mysterious *Portrait of a young Woman* (cat. 2), a painting of clashing colours and disturbing mood. The artist Cristoph Amberger (circa 1502-1562) who spent time in Italy and met Titian, was more in tune with the tastes and demands of the public with his *Portrait of Matthäus Schwarz* (cat. 4), painted with great attention to the small details which conveyed something of the personality of the sitter who was the accountant of the famous Függer family, bankers to Charles V.

28. **Hans Baldung Grien**
*Portrait of a Lady, 1530(?)*

Oil on panel. 69.2 x 52.5 cm

# 10 16th-century Netherlandish Painting

Sixteenth-century Netherlandish painting is generally considered to represent something of a plateau between the high points of the fifteenth and the seventeenth centuries. It is certainly the case that it drew heavily on Italian art of the period in a rather provincial manner. Despite this, the paintings hung in this room amply demonstrate that sixteenth-century Netherlandish art could be both original and finely painted.

The generation of artists born at the end of the fifteenth century introduced the new, Italian-influenced style, for which they were traditionally known as the "Romanists". The oldest and probably the most interesting of these artists was Jan Gossaert (1478-1533/36), sometimes known as Mabuse after his native town of Mabeuge. Gossaert combined the influence of Dürer with that of Michelangelo to create a highly personal and expressive pictorial language, as we can see in his *Adam and Eve* (cat. 163). Other painters influenced by Italian art, particularly Raphael, include Bernaert van Orley (circa 1488-1541), Jan van Scorel (1495-1532) and Joos van Cleeve (circa 1485-1541), all represented in this room.

One of Van Scorel's pupils was the Haarlem painter Maerten van Heemskerck (1498-1574) who travelled to Rome in the 1530s at a time when Michelangelo's fame was again in the ascendent and when Mannerist art had firmly taken root. Heemskerck painted the splendid *Portrait of a Lady spinning* (cat. 183), which dominates the room. Although the painting seems to be the simple representation of an everyday scene it is in fact a complex image in which emblematic imagery drawn from the Bible is mingled with a delight in the depiction of earthly pleasures. Heemskerck brilliantly conveys textures and rich colouring in a manner which looks forward to Dutch painting of the seventeenth century.

One artist worth singling out is Joachim Patinir (circa 1485-1524), one of the most unusual painters of the sixteenth century. In his *Rest on the Flight into Egypt* (cat. 314) the depiction of the tiny holy figures is really only an excuse to represent an extensive landscape with woods and fields painted in a clearly Germanic style. Taken up and transformed by the artists working in Antwerp in the sixteenth century, the biblical and mythological landscapes of Patinir are in fact a distant source for the great landscape paintings of seventeenth-century Holland.

**183. Marten van Heemskerck**
*Portrait of a Lady spinning, c. 1531*

Oil on panel. 105 x 86 cm

# 11 Titian, Tintoretto, Bassano and El Greco

By the mid-sixteenth century Titian was internationally recognised as the most important Venetian, even Italian, painter. Around this date his art underwent a profound change which can probably be associated with his trip to Rome in 1545. His meeting with Michelangelo, who had just completed the great fresco of *The Last Judgement*, seems to have inspired Titian to experiment further in his art. During this Italian trip he painted the *Danäe*, now in the Museo de Capodimonte, Naples, the first of a new series of paintings on mythological themes. Titian justified the freedom with which he treated these themes by explaining that he created them not in the manner of telling a story, but rather of composing a poem. This explanation could also be applied to his new approach to colour. Vasari, who visited the artist's studio in Venice in 1566 described his work thus: "The style he has used in his latest works is very different to those of his youth...they are painted with daring brushstrokes, made with broad, even rough movements of the brush so that, seen from close up, they make little sense, but seen from afar, they come together perfectly (...). This method of painting, used in this way, is judicious, beautiful and astonishing because it makes the pictures seem truly alive and painted with great skill, but without any obvious effort".

While Titian reduced the number of different colours which he used, each colour was broken down into an infinite number of different tones, distributed across the picture space. The result is a blending of figure and background with no neutral areas. His paintings can be likened to the great, musical polyphonic compositions of that time, in which the melodic lines come together to bring out the central theme of the work. In the same way, the various parts of Titian's paintings meld together to create an overall effect in harmony with the nature of the subject matter.

Titian's painting of *Saint Jerome* (cat. 406) was painted in the last years of the artist's life although it repeats a compositional type which he developed twenty years earlier. Alone in the desert, the saint meditates on Christ's Passion. The bundle of branches on the ground and the stone in his hand remind us of his penitence. In the undergrowth the greenish notes of a few leaves echo the shadows which mortify the torso of the old man. His purple robe extends in a zig-zag form along the diagonal which divides the composition. In the lower right hand corner the powerful head of the lion is concealed in the shade, while at the upper left the light becomes

**406. Titian**
*Saint Jerome in the Desert, c. 1575*

Oil on canvas. 135 x 96 cm

## Titian, Tintoretto, Bassano and El Greco

dimmed by the undergrowth. An air of melancholy pervades the living and the inanimate forms alike.

The influence of Titian's late style reached as far as Rubens and Watteau and beyond that to late Cézanne. It is certainly not surprising that it transformed painting in Venice in the second half of the sixteenth century. Titian's late style lies behind the sombre blue tones of the *Pastoral Scene* (cat. 31) by Jacopo Bassano (circa 1515-1592), as does the glorious spiral of light and the heavenly bodies in Tintoretto's *Paradise* (cat. 403, on show in the main atrium).

The art of El Greco (1541-1614) was also strongly influenced by the Venetian style. The composition of his *Annunciation* (cat. 172), painted in Venice, is based on an Annunciation painted by Titian in 1537. The influence of Mannerism on his work is also obvious. The full working out of this Italian influence together with the painter's own personal development following his arrival in Toledo gave rise to one of the most unique pictorial styles in the history of art, a style which reaches its extraordinary culmination around the turn of the century and which had nothing in common with the new artistic trends which were spreading out from Italy at that time. Two examples of El Greco's late style are the splendid small version of *The Annunciation* painted for the altarpiece of the Colegio de la Encarnación in Madrid (cat. 171) and *The Immaculate Conception* (cat. 170).

403. **Tintoretto**
*The Paradise, c. 1583*

Oil on canvas. 164 x 492 cm

**171. El Greco**
*The Annunciation, 1596-1600*

Oil on canvas. 114 x 67 cm

# 12 Caravaggio and the Early Baroque

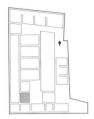

In the last two decades of the sixteenth century Rome reasserted its position as the world's artistic capital. This was due to the birth of a new style, the Baroque, which was to dominate the artistic life of the Catholic cities of Europe throughout the seventeenth century and well into the eighteenth century. The works on show in this room are from the early stages of its development which lasted until the third decade of the seventeenth century.

The arrival of this new style has been explained in terms of stylistic development (by Wölfflin), or in theological terms as a response to the religious tenets of the Counter-Reformation (according to Weisbach). Both the conclusions of the Council of Trent and the propagandistic requirements of the new religious orders (principally the Oratorians and the Jesuits) required that works of art were: 1. clear and easily understandable; 2. an aid to stimulating pious emotions; 3. lifelike or "realistic". These requirements underpin the new artistic style, a style which was opposed to artificiality, to the cold intellectualism and the complexity of late Mannerism.

Even though the art of Caravaggio (1571-1610) responded to the demands of the new taste, it was not by any means universally accepted in its time. This has traditionally been attributed to the fact that his figures were too realistic in presentation, and therefore at odds with the norms of the classical tradition, as well as with the decorum required in the treatment of religious themes. However Caravaggio's paintings frequently remind us less of the real world than of the irreality of the theatre or of a "tableau vivant". In any case, Caravaggio's style could be seen to be well suited to some religious tendencies within the Counter-Reformation which demanded that the decorum and beauty of the work of art be subordinated to the pious emotions that it should arouse. That this tendency failed to become the pre-eminent one in the early seventeenth century explains the rejection of Caravaggio's art in academic circles.

Painted in the last five years of the sixteenth century is the *Saint Catherine of Alexandria* (cat. 81) by the still young Caravaggio. The art historian Wittkower has related this painting to the tradition of Flemish still-life painting whose influence is obvious in Caravaggio's early paintings. There is certainly something of the still-life in the treatment here of the contrasting textures of the brocades which take up a large proportion of the picture surface, and also in the broken wheel, the white of her blouse, the blade of the

81. **Caravaggio**
*Saint Catherine of Alexandria, c. 1597*

Oil on canvas. 173 x 133 cm

# Caravaggio and
# the Early Baroque

sword and her index finger which rests on it. As the art historian Longhi observed, the model's knuckles are surprisingly prominent for a girl with such a delicate throat.

Despite his fame, Caravaggio's ideas were never transmitted though an organised school of followers. The works on show in this room and in room 20 give an idea of the vary varied styles of the artists who became known as the Northern Caravaggisti, from Hendrick Terbrugghen (1588-1629) to Valentin de Boulogne (circa 1591-1632). Even more distinct in style is José de Ribera (1591-1652), a Spanish artist who worked in Rome and Naples. Ribera developed Caravaggio's realism and harsh focused lighting further than any other of his followers. His *Lamentation* (cat. 336) of 1633

415. **Valentin de Boulogne**
*David with the Head of Goliath and two Soldiers, 1620-22*

Oil on canvas. 99 x 134 cm

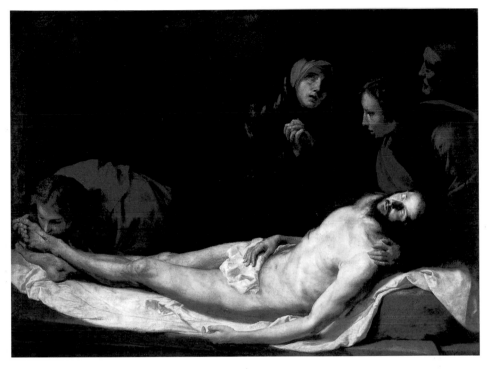

336. **José de Ribera**
*The Lamentation, 1633*

Oil on canvas. 157 x 210 cm

also shows the influence of Van Dyck (who had passed through Palermo) as well as the artist's own maturing powers, and Ribera was to become one the most individual artists of the Baroque period, in Italy and beyond.

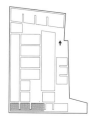

Rooms 13 to 15 are devoted to the art of the new Baroque style whose first appearances are recorded in the paintings in room 12. Caravaggio's art and the rise of a new naturalistic approach are the starting points for these paintings, including works by Salini, Fetti and an artist connected with the city of Naples, Mattia Preti.

Tommaso Salini (circa 1575-1625) was a contemporary and rival of Caravaggio in Rome. His *Young Peasant Boy with a Flask* (cat. 363) is a genre painting, a type of painting of Flemish origin also picked up by Caravaggio in his early compositions. Responding to a new trend, collectors were commissioning scenes of daily life. The new subjects were painted in an equally novel style relying on dramatic effects of light and shade.

Domenico Fetti (1589-1624) might be described as an eclectic painter who combined an interest in the new naturalistic lighting effects with the colouring of the Venetian masters of the sixteenth century. His two small panels, *The Good Samaritan* and *The Parable of the Sower* (cat. 139 and 140) illustrate two stories from

176. **Guercino**
*Christ and the Woman of Samaria at the Well, 1640-41*

Oil on canvas. 116 x 156 cm

327. **Mattia Preti**
*A Concert, c.1630-40*
Oil on canvas. 107 x 145,5 cm

the New Testament. The subjects of the paintings conform with the ideas of the Counter-Reformation.

The new naturalistic style of painting was to become particularly important in Naples, initially due to Caravaggio's presence then thanks to Ribera. One artist with close connections to the city was Mattia Preti (1613-1699), whose *Concert* (cat. 327) is painted in a particularly delicate manner. It represents three people in half-length format grouped around a table against a neutral background. The intense white light which falls on their faces from the side illuminates a very narrow colour range of blacks and earth tones. Preti's interest in these secular subjects dates from his youthful stay in Rome and from contact with northern artists who formed a lively colony in that city in the early decades of the seventeenth century.

Giovanni Francesco Barbieri, known as Il Guercino (1591-1666), is one of the outstanding artists from the second generation of Bolognese Classicism. *Christ and the Woman of Samaria by the Well* (cat. 176) gives us a good idea of his style: the naturalistic presentation of the figures and their setting blends harmoniously with

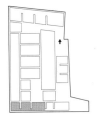

the elegant formal balance of the composition. Guercino's refined colouring, his beautiful rendering of draperies and objects and the delicate handling of light make it easy to understand why he was at one point one of the most sought-after painters of the Roman Baroque.

Painting by French artists at this date had its centres of activity in Rome and Paris. It developed towards a moderated form of the Baroque, always tempered by a leaning towards Classicism. Nonetheless, some artists opted for a more naturalistic mode. This was the case with the Le Nain, a family of three artists, Antoine (1600/10-1648), Louis (1593-1648) and Matthieu (1607-1677), whose generally small-format compositions depict the life of the French peasantry, as in *Children singing and playing the Violin* (cat. 218) on show in room 13.

It was the French artists working in Italy who tended most towards a classicizing style. Claude Gellée (1600-1682), called Lorraine, settled in Rome in 1627. Claude created a type of panoramic landscape which nostalgically evokes the classical world. His *Landscape with the Flight into Egypt* (cat. 226) is typical of his interpretation of the Roman Campagna. The pinkish tones which suffuse the horizon are painted at dusk. In the foreground, painted with a contra-light, the clumps of trees are arranged to frame the scene like the wings of an Italian-style theatrical set. Sébastien Bourdon (1616-1671) also represented the classicizing trend which dominated French art of the seventeenth century. His *Holy Family with Saint Elizabeth and the Infant Saint John the Baptist* (cat. 59) shows the influence of Poussin which was evident in Bourdon's work during the last decade of his life.

The art of Valdés Leal (1622-1690) and Murillo (1617-1682) was a renewed high point in Spanish art in the second half of the seventeenth century, particularly in Seville. *The Virgin and Child with Saint Rosalina of Palermo* (cat. 296) by Bartolomé Esteban Murillo is typical of this great artist's work in the last years of his career. The composition is simple: the triangular arrangement of the figures is set off to the left by a secondary scene depicting an incident from the life of the saint possibly based on a view in Seville. The cherubim and martyrs in the middle ground have been painted with a loose brush, their forms softened by the treatment of light and colour. The painting is a perfect example of Murillo's brilliant and eclectic style, gifted with an easy ability to communicate

296. **Bartolomé Esteban Murillo**
*The Virgin and Child with Saint Rosalina of Palermo, c. 1670*

Oil on canvas. 190 x 147 cm

59

**59. Sébastien Bourdon**
*The Holy Family with Saint Elizabeth and the*
*Infant Saint John the Baptist, c. 1660-70*

Oil on canvas. 39 x 50 cm

religious sentiment that was appreciated not only by his contemporaries and by the prevailing spirit of the late Counter-Reformation, but by much later generations including the Romantics, who viewed his art from a very different cultural perspective.

**226. Claude Lorraine**
*Landscape with the Flight into Egypt, 1663*

Oil on canvas. 193 x 147 cm

# 16-18 18th-century Italian Painting

Italy's pre-eminent position as the centre of the art world was challenged by France, in particular Paris, in the eighteenth century. Nonetheless Italy continued to be an essential destination for artists and aristocrats from all over Europe who travelled there to admire the country's classical ruins and archaeological remains.

In addition to Rome other cities enjoyed something of an artistic renaissance, particularly Venice which made a unique contribution to the artistic panorama. Venice was the birthplace of one of the century's most important artists, Giambattista Tiepolo (1696-1770). *The Death of Hyacinth* (cat. 394) is one of his masterpieces and illustrates one of the stories from Ovid's *Metamorphoses*. The painting perfectly demonstrates Tiepolo's style: the rich colouring based on a highly individual palette in which cool, pale tones predominate, the brilliance of handling, the highly effective organisation of the composition, and the marvellous sense of drama with which the narrative unfolds. An enormously able artist, Tiepolo was commissioned to fresco the ceilings of the palaces of some of the main European courts. Among them was the Royal Palace in Madrid, the city in which he died in 1770.

Although only fourteen years older than Tiepolo, Giovanni Battista Piazzetta (1683-1754) was his teacher. He was also an artist with a unique and highly personal style. His portrait of his pupil, the woman poet and painter *Giulia Lama* (cat. 316), skilfully combines the energy and reduced colour spectrum of the Caravaggist tradition with the intimate mood favoured by the taste of his own time.

The early eighteenth century in Venice saw strong demand for various types of paintings which were developed to new artistic levels. Among the most important of these were "vedute" or view paintings. This genre had existed in the seventeenth century but was influenced by two new factors in the eighteenth century: the enthusiasm for classical ruins and architecture and the developments in theatrical scenery. Both of these are evident in the complicated imaginary architecture of two paintings (cat. 311 and 312) by the Roman painter and architect Giovanni Panini (circa 1691-1765). However, artists were soon depicting real architecture, generally in Rome, Florence and above all Venice. A key factor in the rise of this genre was the patronage of foreign clients, notably the English, who liked to take home souvenirs of their youthful travels in Italy, traditionally known as the "Grand Tour".

**394. Giambattista Tiepolo**
*The Death of Hyacinth, 1752-53*

Oil on canvas. 278 x 235 cm

**63**

# 18th-century
# Italian Painting

Foremost among the view painters was Antonio Canale, known as Canaletto (1697-1768) who trained as a painter of theatrical scenery. Canaletto knew better than any other artist how to convey the magical beauty of Venice in his paintings. Two panoramic views of Venice, *View of the Piazza San Marco* (cat. 75) and *View of the Grand Canal from San Vio* (cat. 76) are painted with his unrivalled precision and skilful perspective. While his canvases are full of bustling human activity, the true protagonists are the architecture, the light and the city.

Painting with a less accurate approach to topography and more poetic freedom were Bernardo Bellotto (1720-1780), a nephew and pupil of Canaletto, and Francesco Guardi (1712-1793), brother-in-law of Giambattista Tiepolo. Bellotto worked in various Italian and German cities before establishing himself at the court of the King of Poland Stanislas Augustus Poniatowski. Displayed here is a beautiful *Idealised view near Padua* (cat. 40), or ideal view, dating from his Italian years.

The large oeuvre of Francesco Guardi (1712-1793) was devoted almost exclusively to Venice. His *View of the Grand Canal*

76. **Canaletto**
*View of the Grand Canal from San Vio, Venice, before 1723*

Oil on canvas. 140.5 x 204.5 cm

75. **Canaletto**
*View of Piazza San Marco, Venice, before 1723*

Oil on canvas. 141.5 x 204.5 cm

*with San Simeone Piccolo and Santa Lucia* (cat. 175), together with its pair (cat. 174) show the city's main canal from two different viewpoints. The loose brushwork creates a variety of effects of which the depiction of light is the most important element. Both Guardi and Bellotto created a type of art that looked forward to the nineteenth century. While Bellotto's luminous compositions suggest Corot's calm and delicate Italian landscapes, the shimmering hazy light of Guardi's Venice anticipates the effects of the Impressionists at the end of the nineteenth century.

Another type of painting which was popular in eighteenth-century Venice was that of scenes of daily life, a genre which had developed in the previous century but which was now particularly admired for its freedom from Baroque rhetoric.

The most outstanding artist in this genre was Pietro Falca (1702-1785), known as Pietro Longhi, whose mainly small-format paintings depict the habits and customs of middle-class and aristocratic Venetians with a lively eye for atmosphere and the significant detail. In *The Tickle* (cat. 224) the spectator peeps in on an intimate

**175. Francesco Guardi**

*View of the Grand Canal with San Simeone Piccolo and Santa Lucia, c. 1780*

Oil on canvas. 48 x 78 cm

family scene which takes place in the salon of a palace. Despite the elegant palette of mainly green tones and a soft brushwork that suggests the French rococo manner, the picture nonetheless exudes a certain feeling of tension or restlessness: its delicate sensibility, almost Rousseauesque, is not in fact so far away from the great outpouring of emotion that characterised the Romantic age which was soon to dawn in Europe.

224. **Pietro Longhi**
*The Tickle, c. 1755*

Oil on canvas. 61 x 48 cm

# 19 17th-century Flemish Painting

In the Low Countries the conflict between the Spanish ruling house and the Protestant world resulted in the separation of Flanders and the Northern Provinces. During the first third of the seventeenth century this process affected art as it did other areas of cultural activity. While Flanders continued to look towards Italy, Dutch painting began to explore other directions (see rooms 20 to 27).

The flowering of Flemish painting at this time was most of all due to Rubens (1577-1640). As with other early Baroque artists, his artistic style is based on a break with Mannerism and a return to the work of the great artists of the first half of the sixteenth century. Rubens synthesised the rich colouring of the Flemish tradition with the drawing and composition of Michelangelo's late period, while the spatial structure of his work derived from Titian's method of constructing space through colour. It is in Rubens's copies of Titian's work that we best see his ability to surpass the art of his time. *Venus and Cupid* (cat. 350) is one of those copies, based on a painting by Titian which had a Neo-platonic theme (ideal beauty reflected in the mirror of love).

In addition to this painting, Rubens is represented in this room by a portrait and two oil sketches. One of these sketches, *The blinding of Samson* (cat. 351) is an outstanding example of Rubens's graphic skills, while the *Portrait of a Woman* (cat. 352) is based on a well-established Flemish prototype, as we can see by comparing it with the *Portrait of Giovanni Battista di Castaldo* (cat. 291), painted half a century earlier by Anthonis Mor (1519-1576), also in this room. The red drapery which fills the background of the picture is a curiously archaic touch, but it is painted with Rubens's characteristically brilliant handling and serves to accentuate the liveliness of gesture and the smooth paintwork in the sitter's face.

The *Portrait of Jacques le Roy* (cat. 135) painted in Antwerp by Van Dyck (1599-1641) in 1631, just before his last trip to England, is the only example in the Thyssen Collection of the work of one of the world's greatest portraitists, but it is outstanding in quality.

Despite the division mentioned above between Dutch and Flemish art, genre painting, which was particularly favoured in Holland, is also found in Flemish art. The same applies to landscape painting and still-lifes. For the sake of visual continuity Flemish paintings of these three types in the Thyssen Museum have

350. **Peter Paul Rubens**
*Venus and Cupid, 1606 12*

Oil on canvas. 137 x 111 cm

# 17th-century
# Flemish Painting

been hung in the same rooms as the Dutch examples. The only exception is with early Flemish landscapes which have been hung in this room to complete the panorama of Flemish art.

The small oil on copper by Jan Breughel the Elder (1568-1625) of *Christ in the Storm on the Sea of Galilee* (cat. 66) was possibly painted in Milan. Nonetheless, it should be seen as one of the very last examples of the interesting tradition of imaginary landscapes which flourished in Flanders in the sixteenth century.

The beautiful pair of landscapes attributed to the so-called "Master of the Monogram IDM" (cat. 288 and 289), probably an artist in the circle of Joos de Momper, are of a compositional type invented by Jan Breughel the Elder. They are good examples of the influence of the Italian style on the art of the Low Countries, a subject which is the theme of room 20. At the same time these paintings represent another step towards the development of the landscape style which flowered in the Golden Age of Dutch art (see rooms 22-26).

135. **Anthony van Dyck**
*Portrait of Jacques Le Roy, 1631*

Oil on canvas. 117.8 x 100.6 cm

# 20-21 17th-century Dutch Painting. Italianate Trends, and Portraits

Dutch seventeenth-century painting was first brought to international attention by enlightened French and English critics of the eighteenth century, particularly those of the period just prior to Romanticism. These critics singled out various characteristics of Dutch painting which they contrasted with those which they saw as typifying Italian art: realism against idealism, sentiment against formalism, and the vernacular against the religious. It was for the historians of the nineteenth century to interpret these characteristics as internally motivated, explaining them as manifestations of the national spirit which had enabled the Dutch people to rebel against Spain and win their independence.

Modern interpretations have rejected these stereotypes and have also modified the traditional distinctions made between Dutch and Flemish art. While we should accept some of these new views only with caution, they are helpful in the case of certain artists like Honthorst and Sweerts whose art very much straddles the middle line between Italian and Dutch, and for that very reason was marginalised by the Romantic critics.

In the present room arrangement, Italianate Dutch painting has been hung next to the room devoted to Rubens and his contemporaries. In order to create a harmonious transition into the Dutch school, a connecting room is devoted to portraits.

The most important Italian influence on Dutch painting is that of Caravaggio. Naturalism, the representation of actions as if frozen at a particularly dramatic moment, and strongly focused light were all introduced into Dutch painting from Italy in the third decade of the seventeenth century and fully assimilated by some Dutch artists into their own work. Utrecht was the main centre for this style and the base for three artists following their return from Italy: Dirk J. van Baburen (circa 1595-1624), whose *Saint Sebastian attended by Saint Irene* (cat. 347) is on show in room 12 (due to its stylistic affinity with Roman art of the time), and Gerrit van Honthorst (1592-1656) whose *Merry Violinist* (cat. 194) is hung in room 22 due to its influence on the development of Dutch genre painting. Hung in room 20 are two paintings of intermediate style. *Esau selling his Birthright* (cat. 393) by Hendrick ter Brugghen (1588?-1629), another artist who worked in Utrecht following his return from Italy, is painted in a very individual style, although with some debt to Honthorst.

*The Supper at Emmaus* (cat. 375) by Matthias Stomer (circa 1600-circa 1650), an artist who spent most of his career in Italy,

**375. Matthias Stomer**
*The Supper at Emmaus, c. 1633-1639*

Oil on canvas. 111.8 x 152.4 cm

**393. Hendrick ter Brugghen**
*Esau selling his Birthright, c. 1627*

Oil on canvas. 106.7 x 138.8 cm

## 17th-century Dutch Painting.
## Italianate Trends, and Portraits

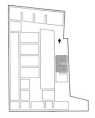

reflects a rather more stereotyped understanding of Caravaggio's art.

A different assimilation of Italian art is to be seen in the work of Bartholomeus Breenbergh (1599-1657). The drawings which he made in Rome in the 1620s served as the basis for the type of imaginary landscape which he produced over the course of a long career. The example on show here (cat. 62) includes a depiction of Michelangelo's statue of *Moses,* as if it were an antique sculpture.

A more interesting artist is Michael Sweerts (1624-1664), a Flemish painter born in Brussels. His *Soldiers playing Dice* (cat. 384) reflects the type of genre painting developed by Dutch artists of the previous generation in Rome, such as Pieter van Laer (circa 1592-1642). The extraordinary *Boy in a Turban* (cat. 385), painted around 1655, is a late but brilliant and very personal interpretation of Caravaggio's style and subject-matter. This link with Caravaggio has prompted a recent interpretation of the picture as an allegory of the sense of smell.

Gerard ter Borch (1617-1681) was one of the last important Dutch artists to travel to Rome. His *Portrait of a Man reading a Document* (cat. 392) takes up Rembrandt's device of setting the sitter within his everyday environment. The artist has achieved his aim with a marvellous treatment of light and a refined palette. Leaving aside Ter Borch and Nicolaes Maes (1634-1693), the other portraits on show in room 21 can be divided into two groups. One group, hung next to a selfportrait (cat. 331) which attribution to Rembrandt, called into doubt during many years, has been lately confirmed, consists of works by contemporaries or followers of Rembrandt, such as Thomas H. de Keyser (1596/97-1667; cat. 209), Govaert Flink (1615-1660; cat. 143), Ferdinand Bol (1616- 1680; cat. 51) and Bartholomeus van der Helst (1613?-1670; cat. 184). The other group, which includes paintings by Caspar Netscher (circa 1635/36-1684; cat. 301 and 302) and Frans van Mieris (1635-1681; cat. 286), indicates a strong shift in taste which took place in Holland in the last decades of the seventeenth century, when Dutch art became much more influenced by the international Classicism which reached Holland via France. As a consequence, Dutch art lost something of its originality.

**392. Gerard ter Borch**
*Portrait of a Man reading a Document, c. 1675*

Oil on canvas. 48 x 39.5 cm

# FIRST FLOOR

# 22-26  17th-century Dutch Painting: Scenes of Daily Life, Interiors and Landscapes

These five rooms bring together paintings devoted to scenes of daily life, interiors, architectural and town views, landscapes and seascapes. Although these types of paintings are found in other countries, they have always been most closely associated with Dutch art, and represent many of its most characteristic features.

Large group portraits of full-length figures, such as the *Family Group* (cat. 179) by Frans Hals (circa 1583-1666), are also characteristic of Dutch painting. The virtuosity of the brushwork and the liveliness and psychological truthfulness of the figures won Hals the admiration of his contemporaries. But in the mid- seventeenth century tastes changed with a marked preference towards more finished pictorial surfaces and Hals was consequently forgotten for two centuries. In the second half of the nineteenth century with the rise of literary and pictorial realism, his work was once again appreciated, and his style was enormously influential on the great precursors of modern painting such as Courbet, Whistler, Manet and Van Gogh.

Although Hals's style was unusual, it was not without precedents, and is probably closest to that of the Utrecht Caravaggisti. Comparing the *Merry Violinist* (cat. 194) by Gerrit van Honthorst (1592-1656), or the *Young Man playing a Lute* (cat. 73) attributed to Jan van Bijlert (circa 1597-1671) with Hals's portraits reveals a similar manner of using theatrical effects, for example the same way of capturing fleeting expressions and gestures (looks, hand movements, or the action of the dog pressing against the girl's dress in the family group). There are also significant differences, in particular the handling of light and perspective which Hals uses to emphasise his naturalistic intentions, in marked contrast to the very focused light and distorted perspective of the Caravaggisti.

It was these differences which set his work apart from the Caravaggisti, leading the painting of scenes of daily life on to new directions to become one of the most distinctive types of Dutch seventeenth-century painting. Nineteenth-century critics, for whom this type of art expressed the essential spirit of the Dutch national genius, saw it as a break with Classicism and as the precursor of modern art. We can now fit it easily into the framework of Classicism as it was understood in the sixteenth and seventeenth centuries in both Holland and Italy. The distinction between the genres of comedy and tragedy, which had its origin in Antiquity, justified certain forms of artistic expression which might be called

179. **Frans Hals**
*Family Group in a Landscape, 1645-48*

Oil on canvas. 202 x 285 cm

"low" and were suitable for describing the characteristic features of reality. Using this "low" genre, which in the theatre corresponded to comedy, the artist could bypass idealisation and the formal requirements which "high" art demanded of him. In painting, the equivalent of "high" art would be paintings of religious or mythological stories, while "low" art would be genre painting. Even if in the modern age critics have rather played down the polarities between Dutch and Italian painting which nineteenth-century critics emphasised, it is certainly the case that the central role of genre painting in Holland gave the art of that country its own character in relation to Italian and international Classicism. Genre painting helped Dutch art on its path towards new stylistic developments in the seventeenth century.

## 17th-century Dutch Painting:
## Scenes of Daily Life, Interiors and Landscapes

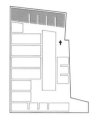

This move towards a different style starts with the art of Adriaen Brouwer (circa 1605-1638), a Flemish artist who moved to Holland and worked in Hals's studio. His *Village Scene* (cat. 65) illustrates the effects of alcohol. It is painted in a satirical and moralising vein influenced by contemporary proverbs and looks back to a type of painting already developed by Peter Breughel the Elder in the sixteenth century. The novelty lies in Brouwer's approach: a completely spontaneous and un-classical composition, an earthy palette tending towards monochrome, and a nervy and irregular brushstroke comparable to the biting line of contemporary genre prints.

Having lived in Holland (in Haarlem and Amsterdam), Brouwer moved to Antwerp. His art influenced that of David Teniers II (1610-1690), a Flemish artist whose huge output contributed to the spread of genre painting in Catholic countries, particularly France and Spain. His brushwork is tighter than Brouwer's

195. **Pieter de Hooch**
*Interior with Woman sewing and a Boy, c. 1662-68*

Oil on canvas. 54.6 x 45.1 cm

**241. Nicolaes Maes**
*The naughty Drummer, c. 1655*

Oil on canvas. 62 x 66.4 cm

and although he also uses a reduced palette, he occasionally allows himself isolated touches of bright colour. Teniers's success was due to his ability to produce varied and interesting compositions (cat. 386 and 387). His work, together with that of his Dutch contemporaries Adriaen van Ostade (1610-1685; cat. 306) and Gerrit Dou (1613-1675; cat. 132) established genre painting and expanded it to satisfy a growing clientele. The stylistic conventions of genre painting were also consolidated at this time. It relied on a set of compositional formulae which could be repeated with certain variants, and also employed a sweeter and more conventional pictorial language. These trends were more evident in the work of the artists of the next generation, such as Gabriel Metsu (1629-1667; cat. 285), Jacob Ochtervelt (1634-1682; cat. 304) and Jan Steen (1625/26-1679). Steen's work often includes theatrical characters or situations, as in his *Self-portrait* (cat. 373) in which the artist presents himself dressed in old-fashioned style theatrical costume.

Genre painting saw a period of innovation in the mid seventeenth century with the work of artists such as Gerard ter Borch, Pieter

# 17th-century Dutch Painting:
## Scenes of Daily Life, Interiors and Landscapes

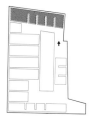

de Hooch and above all Jan Vermeer. Although their contemporaries still read allegorical interpretations into their paintings, such as the opposition between the active and the contemplative life, these artists were less dependent on literary or theatrical sources, and were more interested in a direct depiction of domestic life and in the resolution of purely pictorial problems. *The naughty Drummer* (cat. 241) by Nicolaes Maes (1634-1693) is a good example of this type of painting, but the best examples in these rooms are the paintings by Pieter de Hooch (1629-1684). In his *Interior with a Woman sewing and a Boy* (cat. 195) Hooch concentrates on the treatment of light and on organising the pictorial space through a succession of planes which recede into the picture space. The same preoccupations are found in *The Council Chamber of Amsterdam Town Hall* (cat. 196). De Hooch has resorted to difficult tricks of perspective (such as the exaggeratedly wide angle of vision) in order to heighten the viewer's sensation of actually being inside the room, and he uses colour with the same end. The figures seem to be there simply to give a sense of scale and consistency to the painted space.

When De Hooch arrived in Amsterdam the most famous painter of architectural interiors was Emanuel de Witte (circa1617-1692; cat. 439). However, the most celebrated Dutch painter in this genre was the Haarlem painter Pieter Saenredam (1597-1665). His style could be described as an equal blending of meticulous accuracy and poetic inspiration. Saenredam had a profound knowledge of the rules of perspective and of architecture, using them expressively and with recourse to subtle distortions disguised by objectivity. A contemporary of the Caravaggisti, Saenredam was, like them, a painter of light, albeit in a very different way. *The West Front of the Church of Saint Mary, Utrecht* (cat. 362) is one of his few pictures of the outside of a building. A mosaic of silvery-grey and golden brushstrokes, with occasional touches of pink, greenish-yellow or lead blue, it describes the effect of the soft light of a Dutch midday falling on the stonework of the medieval building.

The transition from architectural and town views to landscapes is another specifically Dutch course of development, and one which, together with genre painting, marked it out as different from other artistic schools.

We can see this development by comparing the *Mountain Landscape* (cat. 365) painted in 1609 by Roelandt Savery (1576-1639) with the *Landscape with armed Men* (cat. 370) by Her-

362. **Pieter Saenredam**
*The West Front of Saint Mary of Utrecht, 1662*

Oil on panel. 65.1 x 51.2 cm

cules Seghers (1589-1633), painted around 1630. Although Flemish by birth and Dutch by training, Savery worked for many years in Prague at the court of Rudolf II, and the *Mountain Landscape* dates from this period. Its literary and fantastical nature can best be understood in the context of the late Mannerist taste which dominated at the Imperial court. Nonetheless the picture

is probably based on sketches made from nature by the artist in the Austrian Tyrol. The painting by Seghers on show here is also an imaginary composition but its literary connotations are less important. The picture's compositional structure, in which the horizon is a flat plane which fades into the distance, framed by a foreground of trees and low hills, was partly invented by the artist. This composition was taken up by many of his contemporaries as it presented a considerable technical challenge. The problem was how to create a feeling of space without resorting to linear perspective: Seghers partly achieved this through his use of colour and partly by deploying the groups of buildings and trees which help to establish successive receding planes. In the case of the painting by Koninck (cat. 211) painted in 1655, we are dealing not with an imaginary but with a real landscape. This is doubly problematic for the artist. In the first place the spectator is familiar with the scene and therefore expects a high degree of accuracy. Secondly, Holland is on the whole a flat country where the horizon is seen low down, obliging the painter to arrange very closely together a series of alternating shady and

370. **Hercules Seghers**
*Landscape with armed Men, c. 1625-35*

Oil on canvas. 36.5 x 54.3 cm

354. **Jacob van Ruisdael**
*View of Naarden, 1647*

Oil on panel. 34.8 x 67 cm

sunny planes which eventually lose themselves on the horizon, and also to handle the colour and paintwork with extreme precision in order to achieve the desired effect of spatial recession.

The simplicity, spontaneity of vision and truthful lighting which the French Impressionists most admired in Dutch painting first made their appearance in the late1630s in the work of the generation of artists born around 1600. These include Jan van Goyen (1596-1656), and Salomon van Ruysdael (circa1600-1670). Van Goyen's *Winter Landscape* (cat. 167) is a good example of his almost monochromatic manner which is sometimes described as "tonal". The literary connotations which the theme of winter had in the sixteenth century (relating to the labours of the months and the seasons) have here lost their importance and have been replaced by the artist's concern with the depiction of space and winter light.

We reach the culmination of Dutch landscape painting with the work of Jacob van Ruisdael (1628-1682), the nephew and pupil of Salomon (who changed the spelling of the family surname). The Thyssen Museum has four of his paintings, of which the *View of Naarden* (cat. 354) is the earliest known work by the artist. Painted when he was nineteen, this remarkable example of realism and delicacy still shows traces of the "tonal" style of Van Goyen and of Salomon van Ruysdael.

The blending of light, colour and space was the greatest contribution of Dutch landscape to the history of painting. In Dutch

seascapes, where the line of the horizon is defined by the meeting between sky and water, these elements are combined with a particular subtlety. Even though the *View of Alkmaar* (cat. 793) by Salomon van Ruysdael is a river view, the representation of space though the modulation of blue, white and grey tones exemplifies the best pictorial values of the Dutch seascape. The picture is a marvel of beauty, simplicity, calm and lightness. The painting by his nephew Jacob, *Stormy Sea* (cat. 359), explores the contrast between the darkness of the turbulent waves and the white of their foam in the stormy light. This painting is probably the one seen by J.M.W. Turner in a London collection one hundred and fifty years later and which, according to his biographer Cunningham, inspired him to paint his own stormy sea which he exhibited at the Royal Academy in 1827 with the title *Port Ruysdael*.

370. **Albert Cuyp**
*Landscape at Sunset, after 1645*

Oil on panel. 48.3 x 74.9 cm

### 793. Salomon van Ruysdael
*View of Alkmaar from the Sea, c. 1650*

Oil on panel. 36.2 x 32.5 cm

# 27 17th-century Still-life Paintings

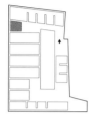

Still-life painting developed as a separate genre at the end of the sixteenth century. Although painted in Italy, France and Spain, it is usually considered to be a particularly Dutch type of painting. In the past historians interpreted the Dutch preference for still-lifes as representing the Calvinist rejection of religious art in favour of a type of painting exclusively devoted to the external appearance of objects, painted with as much accuracy as possible. Seen in this way, still-life painting was a lesson in observation and in painting.

Against this view, recent art history has chosen to emphasise the symbolic aspects of the genre. The most striking example of this is the symbolism which has been found in so-called "Vanitas" paintings. The open watch in paintings by Kalf (1619-1693; cat. 202 and 204), or the broken wine glass in the painting by Heda (1593-1680; cat. 181) may be pointing to the closeness of death. Similarly, the caterpillars and butterflies in the floral still-lifes could allude to time's all-devouring action.

Other types of symbolism can be read into the floral still-lifes. The rare types of flowers painted by A. Bosschaert (1573?-1621) in his *Chinese Vase with Flowers* (cat. 56) reflect his patrons' interest in the natural sciences. The painting should be seen as a sort of botanical portrait painted for the enjoyment of scientists and interested amateurs.

As well as flowers, other forms of collecting developed in seventeenth-century Holland: Chinese porcelain, rugs, goldsmiths' work, and of course paintings. The fact that paintings not only depicted collectible objects but were collectible themselves gives rise to a number of interesting ideas. In the epitaph which the poet Van der Hoeven composed for Kalf he wrote that the artist knew how to paint the richest treasures, but that no treasure would be sufficient payment for his marvellous skill as a painter, praise which was later repeated by Goethe.

The earlier interpretations of still-life saw it as a lesson in how to look and how to paint, but this does not exclude the idea of symbolic interpretation. In a short text on "Vanitas" paintings written at the end of his life, André Chastel compared the table on which the objects in a still-life are arranged with a sacrificial altar: the greater the skill of the artist in painting the freshness of the petals, the softness of the textiles and the variety of reflections on liquids and metals, the more dramatic and effective the painting's role in denouncing the vanity of earthly appearances.

**202. Willem Kalf**
*Still-life with Porcelain and a Nautilus Cup, 1660*

Oil on canvas. 64.1 x 55.9 cm

# 28 18th-century Painting: From Rococo to Neo-Classicism

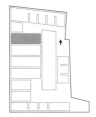

The symptoms of a profound crisis in European culture began to appear around the end of the eighteenth century and the beginning of the nineteenth. One of its consequences was a change in taste which called into question the classical values as upheld by the Academy, namely the primacy of drawing and composition, idealism and the hierarchy of the various genres of painting. Instead of aiming to uplift or edify the spectator, as required by the conventions of classical poetry, the work of art now aimed to appeal to his or her senses and to give pleasure. It is worth noting that the new taste, which was given the rather pejorative label of "Rococo", had its origins in the fields of decoration and genre painting.

The Rococo style spread rapidly from France to the rest of Europe due to the increasingly international nature of the aristocratic lifestyle. Some decades later Neo-Classicism, the new style which developed as a reaction to the Rococo, was transmitted in a similar way, although with greater institutional support. Although in some ways it reinstated the traditional hierarchies, Neo-Classicism was not a straightforward movement: while it defended the values of the Academies, it did so in order to create a new moral and rational underpinning for artistic activity. Linked to the activity of the Encyclopedists, its development formed part of the complex history of the Enlightenment. At the end of the century it was associated with the French Revolution, although elsewhere, for example England, it exhibited certain anti-Revolutionary tendencies. In many places it was connected with the beginnings of the Romantic movement.

The first of the great Rococo artists was Antoine Watteau (1684-1721). The museum has two of his paintings. *The Rest* (cat. 431) forms part of a series of paintings of military scenes which Watteau painted while still very young. *Pierrot Content* (cat. 432) is a garden scene with figures dressed as characters from the *Commedia dell'Arte*. The subject relates to the series of paintings known as "Fêtes galantes" which includes the famous *Embarkation for Cythera* with which Watteau secured his entry into the Académie. Inspired by the paintings of Rubens and Titian, whose works he studied and admired in Paris collections, Watteau's style was profoundly personal and innovative. His followers, who imitated his style but primarily his themes, included Nicolas Lancret (1690-1734), represented in this museum by two paintings (cat. 215 and 216) and Jean-Baptiste Joseph Pater (1695-1736), represented here by a *Concert Champêtre* (cat. 313).

432. **Jean-Antoine Watteau**
*Pierrot Content, c. 1712*

Oil on canvas. 35 x 31 cm

The best example of Rococo painting is perhaps the work of François Boucher (1703-1770), an artist who enjoyed the patronage of Madame de Pompadour. His compositions, painted in bright and pleasing colours, appealed very directly to the collective imagination of his numerous clients. *La Toilette* (cat. 58) is one of his most characteristic works and of the highest quality.

The work of Jean-Baptiste Chardin (1699-1779) was stylistically coherent but was appreciated for very different reasons and

## 18th-century Painting: From Rococo to Neo-Classicism

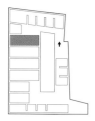

by opposing camps, a situation which reflects the cultural complexity of the eighteenth century. Chardin worked in the Dutch manner (which spread across France at the same time as the Rococo style) but was nevertheless admitted to the Académie in 1728, furthermore for his still-life paintings. Later he was one of the favourite artists of the Encyclopedists. The museum has three of his still-lifes, all from 1728. The *Still-life with Jug and copper Cauldron* (cat. 118) is on show in room 27, along with Dutch painting from the previous century. On show in this room, the *Still-life with Cat and Rayfish* (cat. 120) and its pair (cat. 119) are good examples of the pictorial qualities which Diderot singled out and admired in the artist's work.

Jean-Honoré Fragonard (1731-1806) and Hubert Robert (1733-1808) became friends during their stay in the Academy in Rome in the early 1760s at a time when the influence of Italian art was again beginning to dominate in French painting. Ultimately Robert opted for the classical mode of landscape, as in his *Interior of the Temple of Diana, Nîmes* (cat. 343). Fragonard, who was not particularly interested in the Académie or in official commissions, took up the Rococo style, renewing it though his own very personal interpretation of Venetian art. *The See-saw* (cat. 148), is an important precedent for his famous painting *The Swing* now in the Wallace Collection, London. Both were commissioned by the same client, the baron de Saint Julien.

England at this time was enjoying a period of unprecedented cultural and artistic richness which, in the field of painting, was most obvious in the genre of portraiture.

Sir Joshua Reynolds (1723-1792), founder of the Royal Academy of Arts, was one of the most important art theoreticians of the century. Based on his study of classical art he developed an eclectic style which was among the finest interpretations of Neo-Classicism in European painting. *The Countess of Dartmouth* (cat. 334), an early work, brings to mind Van Dyck's portraits. Johann Zoffany (1733-1810) achieved considerable success with a style which was much more theatrical and spectacular than Reynolds's academic mode. This is obvious in Zoffany's *Portrait of Ann Brown in the role of Miranda* (cat. 444), one of his best known masterpieces. Thomas Gainsborough (1727-1788), the other great artistic figure of the eighteenth century in England, anticipated the picturesque and romantic mood which was to prevail at the end of the century. In his

**120. Jean-Baptiste-Simeon Chardin**
*Still-life with Cat and Rayfish, c. 1728*

Oil on canvas. 79.5 x 63 cm

*Portrait of Sarah Buxton* (cat. 153), one of his most typical portraits, Gainsborough attempts to capture the sitter's state of mind through his depiction of her dress, the landscape and the dominant tones of the painting.

# 29-30 19th-century North American Painting

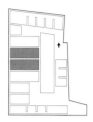

The paintings on show in rooms 29 and 30 encompass a period of art history which is very little represented in Europe's museums. Coinciding with the beginnings of Independence, North American painting of the nineteenth century began to take on its own identity as a national school based on a very individual interpretation of Romanticism. During the Colonial era before Independence, American art was strongly influenced by Britain. The most notable eighteenth-century artist was the British painter John Singleton Copley (1738-1815), whose precisely drawn portraits have preserved for posterity the appearances of some of the most notable figures of the age. The museum has three paintings from his North American period, the *Portrait of Judge Martin Howard* from 1767 (cat. 99), the *Portrait of Miriam Kilby, wife of Samuel Hill* from around 1764 (cat. 98) and the *Portrait of Catherine Hill, wife of Joshua Henshaw II* of 1772 (cat. 97). Among his followers it is worth singling out Charles Wilson Peale (1741-1827), whose *Portrait of Isabella and John Stewart* of around 1775 (cat. 315) follows the British eighteenth-century portrait type.

Following Independence, landscape painting became the best vehicle for the expression of the new Romantic and nationalistic ideals. North American landscape painting of the nineteenth century is characterised by its exaltation of nature, based on the contemporary perception of the American landscape as a new Garden of Eden, a virgin land given to the pioneers as a reward for their struggles.

The earliest and main school of North American landscape painting was known as the Hudson River School. It was founded by Thomas Cole (1801-1848), an artist of English origins. His paintings, *Expulsion. Moon and Firelight* (cat. 95) and *Cross at Sunset* (cat. 96) are examples of a tendency towards symbolism and spiritualism which drew its inspiration from English and German Romanticism. Cole's followers include his only actual pupil Church (1826-1900) and various contemporaries such as Durand (1796-1855), Kensett (1816-1872), Cropsey (1823-1900) and Bierstadt (1830-1902), all represented here. These artists prolonged the tradition of Romantic landscape painting through the whole of the nineteenth century.

Alongside the Romantic school was the Luminist movement which treated landscape in a more lyrical manner. Artists of this school include Martin Johnson Heade (1819-1904) and Fitz Hugh

**91. James Goodwyn Clonney**
*Fishing Party on Long Island Sound off New Rochelle, 1847*

Oil on canvas. 66 x 92.7 cm

**95. Thomas Cole**
*Expulsion. Moon and Firelight, c. 1828*

Oil on canvas. 91.4 x 122 cm

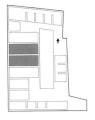

Lane (1804-1865) who painted seascapes and landscapes of the American East Coast.

Another genre which developed alongside landscape was a particularly American form of genre painting. This has two principal aspects: scenes of daily life and paintings inspired by the customs and life of the Native Americans. *Fishing Party on Long Island Sound off New Rochelle* (cat. 91) by James G. Clonney (1812-1867) is a splendid example of the first type. Painted before the War of Succession, it is an idyllic image of North American society at the beginning of the nineteenth century. The paintings of ethnographic subjects were a sort of projection of the buccaneering spirit of the Wild West Frontier pioneers and their colonialist adventure. This form of painting began in the 1840s and continued to evolve into the the twentieth century. In the early days artists painted scenes which they might actually have observed first-hand, for example the painting by George Catlin (1796-1872) called *The Falls of Saint Anthony* (cat. 487). Following the War of Succession and the modernisation of North American society "Indian Paintings" became more and more stereotyped, as we see in the night scene by Frederic Remington (1861-1909), *Apache Fire Signal* (cat. 722).

Another particularly North American type of painting was a style of still-life which was developed at the end of the nineteenth century and the beginning of the twentieth and which is characterised by a minute rendering of reality using trompe l'oeil effects. The museum has four paintings by the best artists of this genre, William M. Harnett (1848-1892) and John F. Peto (1854-1907). In *Materials for a Leisure Hour* (cat. 574) Harnett presents a group of everyday objects painted in a hard style and arranged in a perfectly balanced composition. His follower Peto took this genre to its limits, as we can see in *Tom's River* (cat. 700), a work which uses illusionistic effects such as the painted frame, the hanging string, the shadow of the nails, the remains of the torn-off paper, and the carved lettering, elements which together give the painting a surprising air of unreality.

The realist tendency was developed in the last third of the century when North American artists turned their attention back to Europe. Notable among these was Winslow Homer (1836-1910), whose painting is the North American equivalent of Courbet's realism and the work of the Barbizon School, although his style was

700. **John Frederick Peto**
*Tom's River, 1905*

Oil on canvas. 50.8 x 40.6 cm

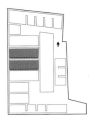

different to that of the French, as we can see in *Waverly Oaks* (cat. 589), an early work which is obviously influenced by Romanticism. In 1883 he moved to Prout's Neck, Maine, from where his paintings reflect the harsh life of the fishermen, the power of the sea and the heroism of man in his struggle with the elements. This is the theme of *The Distress Signal* (cat. 588) from 1880.

From the same generation as Homer, James A. McNeill Whistler (1834-1906) could not be more different. He represents the uprooted American artist who settled in Europe and worked in London and Paris. His taste for Japanese art is reflected in the simplicity and subtlety of his colouring and composition. From 1870, Whistler concentrated more on portraiture. His painting *Pink and gold: the Neapolitan* (cat. 784) is a good example of his virtuoso paintwork and the refinement of his colouring. As well as Whistler, the influence of Japanese art is evident in the work of William Merritt Chase (1849-1916), represented here by *Shinnecock Hills* (cat. 502) and *The Kimono* (cat. 501).

Finally we arrive at the work of John Singer Sargent (1856-1925), an artist born in Florence to American parents who spent much of his life in Venice, Paris, London and other European cities. Sargent admired the art of Hals and Velázquez and was also influenced by Impressionist painting. From his Venetian period is *The Venetian Onion Seller* (cat. 731), a painting notable for its loose brushwork and interest in the effects of light. In it we can see how close Sargent's style was to that of the Spanish painter Sorolla, who became a close friend. Sargent achieved great fame as a portrait painter of the English aristocracy and the American upper classes. His *Portrait of Millicent, Duchess of Sutherland* (cat. 732) is a typical example of one such portrait.

502. **William Merritt Chase**
*Shinnecock Hills, 1893-97*

Oil on panel. 44.4 x 54.6 cm

591. **Winslow Homer**
*Portrait of Helena de Kay, c. 1873*

Oil on panel. 31 x 47 cm

# 31 19th-century European Painting: From Romanticism to Realism

Looked at through the critical filter of our own time, the art of the nineteenth century seems to us to herald the dawn of modern art. Thus we see Impressionism as the first modern art movement and the rest of the century as containing the elements which led up to it: the anti-classical rebellion of the Romantic and Realist movements, and the realist doctrine which placed pictorial expression within the realm of the senses.

Although biased, this interpretation has some truth to it: the history of art has set up many similar scenarios, starting with Vasari, who explained the art of the fourteenth and fifteenth centuries in relation to the sixteenth-century Renaissance.

However it may be, if we accept the thesis that the art of the Enlightenment is linked to that of the twentieth century via Romanticism, Realism and Impressionism, no artist could act as a better source and guide to this process of evolution than Goya (1746-1828). The three paintings in the museum are from his mature period. Notable for its delicacy and daring is the portrait of *Asensio Juliá* (cat. 166). The sitter was a Valencian painter and a friend of Goya's who worked with him on the frescoes of San Antonio de la Florida in Madrid. *El Tío Paquete* (cat. 165) is a small painting from the same period as the artist's "Black Paintings", made just before the artist went into exile in Bordeaux where he spent the rest of his life.

While Theodore Géricault (1791-1824) was an artist of the early Romantic movement in France, his painting deliberately evokes the monumentality of classical sculpture. His *A Scene from the free Horse Race* (cat. 157) is a good example of this. Fully Romantic in conception and execution are the two small oils by Delacroix (1798-1863), *Arab Rider* and *The Duke of Orléans revealing his Lover* (cat. 126 and 127).

Caspar David Friedrich (1774-1840) was the chief artist of German Romanticism, a movement diametrically opposed to French Romanticism. *Easter Morning* (cat. 792) is a relatively late work in the artist's most pared down and simplified style. Friedrich's work was profoundly innovative, the only precedents perhaps to be found in some Dutch seventeenth-century art. Friedrich, however, dispensed with the interdependence of space and light in order to make light the main element, representing for him the unity of nature. Friedrich's art had little direct influence outside his circle of friends and pupils. However, as the art histori-

**166. Francisco de Goya**
*Asensio Julià, c. 1798*

Oil on canvas. 54.5 x 41 cm

**792. Caspar David Friedrich**
*Easter Morning, 1833*

Oil on canvas. 43.7 x 34.4 cm

an Robert Rosenblum has argued, his painting lies at the origins of a specifically Nordic and modern artistic tradition centred on the notion of the Sublime, which lasted through the nineteenth and into the twentieth century, reaching as far as artists such as Rothko (see room 46).

One of the key ideas of Romanticism was that nature was a unified whole in which the sum was greater than the individual parts. This idea continued to be expressed, albeit in a modified way, in the successive waves of Realist and Naturalist styles which arose during the century. Gustave Courbet (1818-1877) made Realism into a political manifesto. *The Stream at Brème* (cat. 495) was painted after Courbet had lost most of the political and artistic battles which he had engaged in. The artist invites us to lose ourselves in his company in the wood where he had passed the summers of his childhood and adolescence.

Camille Corot (1796-1875) is an artist difficult to classify. A Romantic, a Classicist and a Realist, the Impressionists considered him a forerunner to their own art. He was the principal artist of the so-called Barbizon School, a movement which was founded on a rejection of the Academy, the study of and return to nature and a direct representation of the landscape. In *Setting out for a Walk in the Parc des Lions* (cat. 494), painted during one of his last summers, the distant still figures of some boys between the trees (the sons of a friend of Corot's) are lit with the silvery light of the Ile de France which was to fascinate Pissarro and his contemporaries.

494. Jean-Baptiste-Camille Corot
*Setting out for a Walk in the Parc des Lions, Port-Marly, c. 1872*

Oil on canvas, 78 x 65 cm

Impressionism began with the *Salon des Refusés* which was founded in 1863 to provide an exhibition venue for artists whose work had been rejected by the official Salon. From that date onward the Impressionists maintained a systematic opposition to academic art. Critics at the time and many later art historians have seen Impressionism as the end of one historical cycle—that of classical art—and the beginning of another one—the era of modern art. However it has to be said that many of the ideas and a good number of the aesthetic formulae of Impressionism were derived from nineteenth-century Realism. There were other antecedents in the art of Turner and Constable and more distant sources such as seventeenth-century Dutch landscape painting or Venetian art, from late Titian to Guardi.

So what, then, was the Impressionist revolution? Firstly, it was a rejection of historical, mythological and religious subject matter. The importance of this lies in the accompanying rejection of the idea of two types of artistic expression: a "formal" manner reserved for elevated public subjects, and an "informal" manner for all other subjects. The hierarchy behind this division was an essential component of the classical system of the arts which remained in force through its application in academic and official circles right through the nineteenth century. The key Impressionist themes such as landscape and the depiction of urban daily life indicate a deliberate preference for the "commonplace" as opposed to the "weightiness" of official art. This preference indicates their first sign of modernity.

The second aspect of the Impressionist revolution concerned its pictorial language. Impressionist artists rejected academic rules in favour of the freshness of personal invention, and substituted the requirements of composition and form (possibly the key elements of the classical mode of painting) for the demand that the painter should recreate the sensations of light and colour which he or she perceived with his/her own eyes. In this way light became the key element in the picture, to the point where some Impressionist painters, for example Monet in his celebrated series of Rouen Cathedral, repeated the same subject seen at different times of the day.

From 1874, the date of their first collective exhibition, the Impressionists formed themselves into an organised and coherent group. It broke up in the second half of the 1880s as the artists of the group became increasingly famous individually.

**659. Edouard Manet**
*Woman in a Riding Habit, full-face, c. 1882*

Oil on canvas. 73 x 52 cm

**712. Camille Pissarro**
*Afternoon on the rue St. Honoré.*
*Effect of Rain, 1897*

Oil on canvas. 81 x 65 cm

**724. Pierre-Auguste Renoir**
*Woman with a Parasol in a Garden, c. 1873*

Oil on canvas. 54.5 x 65 cm

# Impressionist and
# Post-impressionist Painting

The museum's collection includes work by the main Impressionist artists. Edouard Manet (1832-1883) should be singled out first. Older than the artists who formed the Impressionist group, Manet was never a formal part of the movement but he is generally considered a forerunner. More than any other artist it was Manet who was responsible for the new emphasis on themes from daily life; however, he was never convinced of the necessity to invent a completely new pictorial language. Manet's art drew on the history of painting, albeit in a very selective way, with a preference for Velázquez, Hals and Goya. In his *Woman in a Riding Habit, full-face* (cat. 659), painted one year before his death, the treatment of light is Impressionist, but the marked contrast between the background and the figure, and the looseness of the brushstroke are reminiscent of Hals and signal the difference between Manet and the Impressionists.

Edgar Degas (1834-1917) had a similar attitude to Manet at times. Degas stood apart from the other members of the Impressionist group due to the importance which he attached to drawing, and because he accepted the primacy of the classical tradition of painting. On the other hand, no other Impressionist artist understood the character of the modern city as well as he, nor the significance of modern urban living for the mood and style of the fin-de-siècle. With the remoteness but obsession of the *voyeur* he often used photography to analyse the effects of daily labours on the bodies of seamstresses, laundry-maids, dancers, sportsmen, and others. His *Swaying Dancer* (cat. 515) belongs to a series on the ballet begun in 1876. Degas makes full use of the unique form of the theatrical stage to experiment with the picture's spatial construction: while the ballerinas waiting in the wings are presented face-on, the ones who are dancing seem to occupy a different spatial plane which the spectator looks down on as if viewing the scene from a box in the audience. Degas reinforces the distortion of the space by framing it in the manner of a snapshot (or a Japanese print), and by cutting off the group of dancers so that only the last one in the line is fully visible. We can only see part of the legs of the one next in line, while the next is just a swirl of gauze. The real theme of the picture are these billows of drapery, sprinkled with the sparkle of the sequins, these artificial green and white creatures who emerge from a dark background where bodies and shadows mingle together, as in the paintings of Watteau or Titian.

515. **Edgar Degas**
*Swaying Dancer, 1877-79*

Pastel on paper. 66 x 36 cm

# Impressionist and Post-impressionist Painting

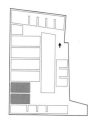

Both the works by Degas in the museum's collection are in pastel. Invented at the end of the eighteenth century, pastel can achieve a purity of colour not possible in any other medium, but it requires extremely brilliant handling otherwise the results are often banal. Degas' complete mastery of the medium is obvious both in the precision of drawing and in his ability to convey the most rich and delicate textures. The reflections of the feathers and materials which fill the pictorial surface of *At the Milliners* (cat. 516) make this work one of Degas' masterpieces.

Claude Monet (1840-1926) took the opposite approach to Degas in systematically rejecting the traditional canons of art. His style gradually abandoned drawing, composition, perspective and volume in order to focus itself entirely on graduations of light and the qualities of colour. *The Thaw at Vétheuil* (cat. 680) belongs to a series of views of the Seine begun in 1878, when Monet had fully worked out his own pictorial language. By applying contiguous brushstrokes of contrasting colours, the artist succeeded in reproducing the effect of winter light on ice and on moving water with extraordinary accuracy.

Close to Monet's art is that of Pierre-August Renoir (1841-1920). *Woman with a Parasol* (cat. 724) is a landscape painted in the summer of 1873. At that time Renoir was working in Giverny with Monet who was painting subjects similar to the ones discussed here. In these paintings we can see the technical issues which interested the Impressionists during this early period of their development. The short, rapid brushstrokes in bright colours turn the picture surface into an unbroken texture of dots and lines. The optic vibrations triggered off by this painted surface create the impression of seeing a sunlit garden of flowers.

Landscape was the Impressionists' favourite genre. This preference represented their closest link with the rest of nineteenth-century painting; it also allowed less innovative artists such as Eugène Boudin (1824-1898; cat. 476) to be considered Impressionist. Pissarro (1830-1903) also dedicated himself almost exclusively to landscape painting. His extensive oeuvre rarely features the type of brilliant and daring compositions for which Monet and Renoir were famous. Pissarro is a painter's painter, sensitive to what interested other artists and also capable of influencing their work. The museum has two of his paintings. *The Wood at Marly* (cat. 711) was painted in the early 1870s at the outset of the Impressionist

**680. Claude Monet**
*Thaw at Vétheuil, 1881*

Oil on canvas. 60 x 100 cm

**516. Edgar Degas**
*At the Milliner's, c. 1883*

Pastel on paper. 75.9 x 84.8 cm

## Impressionist and
## Post-impressionist Painting

movement and is still very close to the style of the Barbizon School. *Afternoon on the rue Saint-Honoré. Effect of Rain* (cat. 712) belongs to a series of views of Paris painted at the end of his life which had a considerable influence on painting at the time. The freshness of the light bathed in the drizzle which falls on the street is typically Impressionist, however the geometrical structure of the composition shows Pissarro's affinity at this date with the work of the young Post-impressionist artists.

The last Impressionist group exhibition took place in 1886. As the group started to disintegrate no other movement with a similarly defined programme attained such a position of dominance. Art historians have applied the term Post-impressionist to the art which was produced in Paris during the last years of the nineteenth century and the beginning of the twentieth century. The most notable artistic trends at this period were Symbolism and Neo-im-

557. **Vincent van Gogh**
*Stevedores in Arles, 1888*

Oil on canvas. 54 x 65 cm

pressionism. Symbolism, which found its most coherent expression through the medium of poetry, was, as far as the visual arts were concerned, more a reflection of a widely-held taste than an artistic style or organised movement. Neo-impressionism was only a defined movement in the early 1890s when it had very little influence; paradoxically it was more important for its influence on the young artists working at the start of the next century (the Fauve and Expressionist painters) than for its own artists (apart from Seurat, who died very young in 1891).

Paul Gauguin (1848-1903) should be considered an independent artist even though his work has some affinities with Symbolism. *Man on the Road (Rouen)* (cat. 552) of 1885 is still painted in an Impressionist style close to that of Pissarro. In 1891 Gauguin left Europe to live in Polynesia. His work there evokes a primitive world as yet uncontaminated by modern man, in which

559. **Vincent van Gogh**
*"Les Vessenots", Auvers, 1890*

Oil on canvas. 55 x 65 cm

# Impressionist and
# Post-impressionist Painting

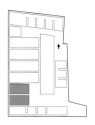

the union between man and nature takes on the value of a spiritual experience. Gauguin was one of the artists whose work had most influence on the next generation, partly because of his evocation of the primitive and partly for his pictorial language which was based on the use of glowing, unrealistic colours and an absence of perspectival depth.

If Gauguin's primitivism is a symptom of the tragic conscience of modernity which developed in artistic and cultural circles at the turn of the century, then the fate of Van Gogh (1853-1890) is its living incarnation. The museum has three of his canvases, painted during different periods of his short career. The earliest (cat. 788) was painted in 1885 when Van Gogh was working in Nuenen in Holland. A letter written by the artist to his brother Theo that year includes the passage: "one of the most beautiful things in this century has been to paint darkness which is also colour". The drama of this landscape at dust, still post-Romantic in mood, contains the germ of the fiery sunset in *Stevedores in Arles* (cat. 557), painted three years later at the beginning of his fruitful period in Provence. *'Les Vessenots', Auvers* (cat. 559) has the typically hallucinatory brushwork of the landscapes painted in Auvers-sur-Oise in the last years of Van Gogh's life.

Henri de Toulouse-Lautrec (1864-1901) is, like Van Gogh, an artist belonging to no particular group or trend; however his Baudelairean talent places him at the opposite extreme to Van Gogh. His ironic and stylised vision of the modern city had a profound influence on the young artists of the early years of the twentieth century, including Picasso. The museum has two of his portraits: one of a friend, *Gaston Bonnefoy* (cat. 773), the other of one of his habitual models, nicknamed *The Redhead* (cat. 774). In this beautiful work, painted in 1889 when Impressionism was disappearing as a movement, the painter was still aiming to capture the effects of light; however the thickness of the brushwork and the construction of the volume through planes suggests Cézanne's search for a style which would bring together the modernity of Impressionism with the solidity of the art of the classical tradition.

It was this synthesis which was to make Paul Cézanne (1839-1906) the nineteenth-century artist who most influenced the art of the twentieth century. For the first half of his career his style was close to that of Impressionism, but the works which have earned him his place in the history of art date from 1890 onwards. *Portrait*

774. **Henri de Toulouse-Lautrec**
*The Red-head in a white Blouse, 1889*

Oil on canvas. 59.5 x 48.2 cm

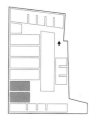

*of a Peasant* (cat. 488) is a magnificent example of the artist's late style. The light which bathes the figure has all the immediacy and luminosity of the best Impressionist paintings, but Cézanne uses colour to construct rather than to dissolve the volumes. It is this development which was to make Cézanne's late work the starting point for Braque and Picasso in their Cubist adventure. While the Impressionists took up that thread of Venetian art which had passed down through Watteau and Turner, Cézanne seems to turn directly back to the message of Titian and the High Renaissance. In doing so, he opened the gates to the new century.

**488. Paul Cézanne**
*Portrait of a Peasant, 1901-06*

Oil on canvas. 65 x 54 cm

# 34 Fauve Painting

The new century dawned with a series of movements which represented the avant-garde until the arrival of Cubism. Fauve painting in France and Expressionism in Germany are the most important of these.

These two movements share the following characteristics: 1. The influence of Post-impressionist artists, primarily Gauguin and Van Gogh; 2. The use of colour for symbolic or emotional ends; 3. An expressionist conception of artistic creation which sees it as the externalisation of the artist's emotional energies; 4. A rebellious attitude towards bourgeois society which often led to an overt sympathy with Anarchism.

Fauvism was born in 1905 following the decision by a group of young French artists whose work had been following similar lines over the past two or three years to show their works together in the Salon d'Automne. Joining forces had the effect of furthering the innovative nature of their work and the group show was one of the biggest scandals to hit the Parisian art world since the start of the Impressionist movement. The art critic Louis Vauxcelles gave the young artists the ironic title of "fauves" (wild animals), but the name stuck as it seemed an apt characterisation of their pictorial style. The Fauves were never an organised group and the movement had a short life, breaking up from 1907.

The movement's leading figure was Henri Matisse (1869-1954). *Yellow Flowers* (cat. 664) on show in room 35 was painted in 1902 before the Fauve group existed. The spatial construction and the use of colour recall Degas' pastels. Along with Matisse, André Derain (1880-1954) and Maurice Vlaminck (1876-1958) formed what the art historian John Elderfield called "the essential triangle of Fauvism". Derain's *Waterloo Bridge* (cat. 524) is one of the most brilliant examples of Fauve painting at its height. It belongs to a series of views of London which Derain was commissioned to paint by the art dealer Vollard in 1905-1906. In them the young artist tried to emulate, albeit in a very different style, Monet's series of London views painted between 1899 and 1903 which had enjoyed considerable commercial and critical success. The influence of Van Gogh and of the Neo-impressionists is obvious, but the painting radiates an impersonal, purely physical energy which places it within the twentieth century.

**524. André Derain**
*Waterloo Bridge, 1906*
Oil on canvas. 80.5 x 101 cm

**664. Henri Matisse**
*Yellow Flowers, 1902*
Oil on canvas. 46 x 54.5 cm

# 35-40 Expressionist Painting

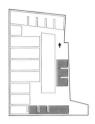

Expressionism was a broad movement, a collective state of mind which had connections with Symbolism and which lasted, albeit with various shifts and changes, through the whole of the first half of the twentieth century.

It rests on one basic supposition: that the work of art exists to express a feeling or emotion rather than give an account of the reality of things. In contrast to Impressionism which always remained linked to sensations and to the outward appearance of the world, for Expressionism the artist's interior vision was paramount. From a stylistic point of view it meant an emphasis on colour over drawing and an accentuated distortion of forms.

The works on show in rooms 36 to 40 include paintings from all the main centres of German Expressionism: Dresden, Berlin and Munich. Room 35 shows work by non-German artists whose work had affinities with Expressionism.

The Norwegian painter Edvard Munch (1863-1944) was an important influence on the work of the Dresden and Berlin artists. *Dusk. Laura, the Artist's Sister* (cat. 689) is a very early work, suffused with the poetic symbolism of the fin-de-siècle: the feeling of isolation and depression which surrounds the woman seated in the foreground is echoed by the light and the colour of the landscape. *The Theatre of Masks* (cat. 534) by Munch's contemporary the Belgian artist James Ensor (1860-1949) deploys a brilliant and acid colouring and a line which dissolves the forms, making them less real and at the same time more expressive.

In turn-of-the-century Vienna Expressionism was taken up by the artists of the generation following the Sezession, such as Egon Schiele (1890-1918) and Oskar Kokoschka (1886-1980). While both took their starting point from Klimt, they moved away from the linear fluidity and decorative nature of his work. The network of vertical and horizontal lines which creates the structure of Schiele's *Houses next to the River. The Old City* (cat. 739) has two functions: a formal one, in that it accentuates the flatness of the picture's spatial structure; and an expressive one, reinforcing the impression of decay which the artist associates with this urban landscape. In Kokoschka's large output his landscapes and portraits were particularly outstanding. In his *Portrait of Max Schmidt* (cat. 629) the rapid brushstroke and the contortion of the hands derive from Van Gogh. The almost hysterical intensity of these elements is characteristic of Kokoschka's early works.

739. **Egon Schiele**
*Houses next to the River. The Old City, 1914*

Oil on canvas. 100 x 120.5 cm

689. **Edvard Munch**
*Dusk. Laura, the Artist's Sister, 1888*

Oil on canvas. 75 x 100.5 cm

# Expressionist Painting

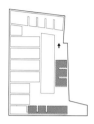

The first formal group set up by the German Expressionist artists was called The Bridge (*Die Brücke*). It started in Dresden in 1905, the year in which Fauvism began in Paris. The first members were four young architecture students: Ernst Ludwig Kirchner, Erich Heckel, Karl Schmidt-Rottluff and Fritz Bleyl. *Die Brücke* was a particularly unified and coherent group. In their search for a common pictorial language the members worked together, sharing their studios, their models and their clients.

The closest collaboration was that between Karl Schmidt-Rottluff (1884-1976) and Erich Heckel (1883-1970). Until 1912 the two artists spent long summers painting together in Dangast, Oldenburg, near the North Sea. Schmidt-Rottluff's *Autumn Landscape in Oldenburg* (cat. 742) and Heckel's *The Brick Factory, Dangast* (cat. 579) are examples of the collective style of the *Die Brücke* artists before 1911. The palette of greens, reds, yellows and bright blues in these pictures derives largely from Van Gogh.

Ernst Ludwig Kirchner (1880-1938) was undoubtedly the most important artist of the group. *Doris in a high Collar* (cat. 613) shows the influence of the Neo-impressionists together with that of Van Gogh. *Fränzi in front of a carved Chair* (cat. 789) reflects the artist's interest in primitive art. The model Fränzi, whose face appears in the foreground, was an eleven year-old girl who regularly posed for Kirchner and other members of the group. Here she is placed on a wooden seat carved by Kirchner himself, the back of which is in the form of an African mask. One striking feature is the contrast between the green tones of Fränzi's face and the pink tones of the African mask.

In 1911 the members of *Die Brücke* moved to Berlin. From that date their paintings used a simplified palette and an increased distortion of spatial construction which completely departed from the rules of perspective. This is the period of *Summer in Nidden* (cat. 699) by Max Pechstein (1881-1955) who joined the group in 1906. In 1914 he travelled to the Palau Islands in Oceania and *Summer in Nidden* reflects the increased orientation towards primitivism evident in his work after this trip. Two works by Kirchner date from this period: *The Bay* (cat. 618), an important pre-War landscape, and *Berlin Street Scene* (cat. 614) which forms part of a series of urban landscapes painted in Berlin between 1913 and 1914. From 1917 Kirchner lived in Switzerland where he developed a still more violent pictorial language, as in his *Alpine*

742. **Karl Schmidt-Rottluff**
*Autumn Landscape, Oldenburg, 1907*

Oil on canvas. 76 x 97.5 cm

579. **Erich Heckel**
*The Brick Factory, Dangast, 1907*

Oil on canvas. 68 x 86 cm

## Expressionist
## Painting

*Kitchen* (cat. 616). The distortion of the space in the picture creates a feeling of agitated movement with the Alpine view in the distance the only fixed point in the painting.

Emil Nolde (1867-1956) joined *Die Brücke* in 1906 on the invitation of Schmidt-Rottluff, but he left in the same year to pursue his own artistic aims. *Summer Clouds* (cat. 691) is a stormy seascape with the clouds and waves treated as solid masses in movement. Nolde's style, based on an expressive use of colour and a feeling of almost religious immersion in nature, varied little throughout his career, as can be see in *Autumn. Dusk* (cat. 690) from 1924 and *Sunflowers* (cat. 692) of 1936.

In 1913 Die Brücke began to break up. One year later an almanac entitled *The Blue Rider* (*Der Blaue Reiter*) was published in Munich by Kandinsky and Marc. A group of international artists all of whom had contacts with the Paris avant-garde associated themselves with this publication (including Kandinsky, Marc, Macke, Jawlensky, Feininger, Itten, V. Burliuk and Klee). Influenced by the German idealist tradition, the artists of the group, particularly Kandinsky, believed that the role of modern art was to free itself

687. **Otto Mueller**
*Female Nudes in a Landscape, c. 1922*

Oil on hessian. 100 x 138 cm

789. **Ernst Ludwig Kirchner**
*Fränzi in front of a carved Chair, 1910*

Oil on canvas. 71 x 49.5 cm

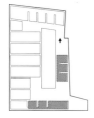

from its dependence on the external world in order to express the world of the spirit, in a way similar to music.

Russian by origin, Wassily Kandinsky (1866-1944) moved to Munich in 1896 where he remained until his return to Russia in 1914. His discovery of abstract painting in 1910 has made him one of the most important artists of the twentieth century. The abstract paintings by Kandinsky in the museum are on show in room 45, while in this room we can see his *Murnau. The Johannisstrasse* (cat. 611). The painting belongs to an experimental period in his work when he was attempting to synthesise Post-impressionism, Fauvism and Expressionism.

*The Dream* (cat. 660) by Franz Marc (1880-1916) is a good example of the spiritualism which characterised The Blue Rider group's work. Marc created a very individual pictorial world in which animals represent beauty, purity and truth. He also worked

691. **Emil Nolde**
*Summer Clouds, 1913*

Oil on canvas. 73.3 x 88.5 cm

616. **Ernst Ludwig Kirchner**
*Alpine Kitchen, 1918*
Oil on canvas. 121.5 x 121.5 cm

out a complex theory which ascribed particular symbolic virtues to colours: blue represented the idea of the masculine, austere and spiritual, to which he opposed yellow as feminine, happy and sensual, and red, symbolising base matter. Mixing these colours resulted in a mingling of these characteristics.

## Expressionist Painting

The early work of Alexej von Jawlensky (1864-1941), a Russian painter who moved to Paris in 1905, reflects the influence of
Matisse with whom he worked for a short time. In 1909 Jawlensky
joined The Blue Rider in Munich. *The Red Veil* (cat. 603) is influenced by Fauve painting but also, in the frontality and calmness of
the female subject, by Russian icons. August Macke (1887-1914)
was of all the artists of the group perhaps the most influenced by
Paris. *Galloping Hussars* (cat. 655), shows the temporary influence
of the Italian Futurists, while *Circus* (cat. 656) was painted just after his trip to Paris in 1912 when he met Delaunay. It shows
Macke's development of an individual style which he deployed until his early death in the First World War in September 1914. Lyonel
Feininger (1871-1956) was another Blue Rider artist who was influenced by the Parisian avant-gardes. The museum owns several
of his works. In *Architecture (The Man from Potin)* (cat. 545) and
*Lady in Mauve* (cat. 543) the juxtaposition of planes has affinities
with Cubism. Johannes Itten (1888-1967) was an independent
Swiss Expressionist painter who taught at the Bauhaus in the 1920s.
*Group of Houses in Spring* (cat. 602) is constructed from a combination of circles, triangles and geometric forms, an example of the
application of the principals of musical composition to painting.

The art of Max Beckmann (1881-1950) occupies a unique
place in the history of twentieth-century art. From 1912 he abandoned Expressionism and turned to Realist painting, inspired by the
great German tradition of the Late Gothic and the art of
Grünewald. Later his work came close to the mood of the New Objectivity (Neue Sachlichkeit) art which criticised German society.
From then on his most important work was the series of allegorical
canvases painted with enormous pictorial and expressive force.
The museum has three paintings which well illustrate his artistic
development. *Self-portrait* (cat. 465) of 1908 is still close to turn-of-
the-century artists like Corinth and Liebermann. *Quappi in a pink
Sweater* (cat. 464) is a portrait of the artist's second wife Quappi
(Mathilde von Kaulbach) whom Beckmann often painted. Here she
is presented frontally, radiating a sort of cheerful tranquillity. *Still-
life with yellow Roses* (cat. 463) shows the artist's interest in pur-
suing problems of colour.

The last phase of German Expressionism is known as New
Objectivity (Neue Sachlichkeit). The movement was a response to
the climate of crisis in post-War Berlin, the scene of the economic,

660. **Franz Marc**
*The Dream, 1912*
Oil on canvas. 100.5 x 135.5 cm

656. **August Macke**
*Circus, 1913*
Oil on cardboard. 47 x 63.5 cm

## Expressionist Painting

political and moral collapse of Bismark's Germany. By using urban subject-matter artists could express a politically or socially critical attitude. As a reaction against the subjective nature of Expressionism, they developed an objective style which aimed at clarity and precision. New Objectivity coincided with the return to figuration which took place in the rest of Europe in the 1920s (see room 45), and involved a similar re-evaluation of Renaissance art, in this case German.

Portrait painting was very popular with the Neue Sachlichkeit artists. In room 40 we find some good examples. *The Portrait of Dr. Haustein* (cat. 733) of 1928, and *Maria and Annunziata from the Port* (cat. 734) of 1923 are by Christian Schad (1894-1982), one of the most obsessively detailed artists of the movement. Two works by Rudolf Schlichter (1890-1955), *Portrait of an Oriental Journalist* (cat. 741), and Albert Henrich (1899-1971), *Portrait of the Painter A. M. Tränkler* (cat. 582) are closer to the expressive naturalism of the pre-War period. *The Double Portrait of Hilde II* (cat. 596) by Karl Hubbuch (1891-1980) is the left half of a canvas which depicts four different aspects of the same model. The canvas was divided up by Hubbuch himself in the 1950s.

The two most important artists of the New Objectivity movement were Otto Dix (1891-1969) and George Grosz (1893-1959). Grosz was a politically active artist and a great draughtsman. The museum has one of his most famous works, *Metropolis* (cat. 569), depicting a view of city streets with a crowd running in all directions. The painting, conceived like a huge collage, has obvious Cubist and Futurist influences, but unlike the Futurist glorification of the city, Grosz's vision is markedly apocalyptic.

In the post-War period Grosz and the other Berlin avant-garde artists allied themselves with the various revolutionary political movements which unsettled German society at that time. This led many of them to adopt a satirical realist style which was intended to be easily comprehensible. The museum has important works on paper, as well as an oil on canvas, *Street Scene. (Kurfürstendamm)* (cat. 572) which illustrate this tendency in Grosz's work.

Dix's work reached maturity in a series of detailed portraits, of which one of the best examples is the *Portrait of Hugo Erfurth with a Dog* (cat. 525). Dix's style was based on that of the German Renaissance painters, not just formally but also in his use of tempera on panel.

464. **Max Beckmann**
*Quappi in a pink Sweater, 1935*

Oil on canvas. 105 x 73 cm

525. **Otto Dix**
*Hugo Erfurth with a Dog, 1926*
Tempera and oil on panel. 80 x 100 cm

New Objectivity came to an end when the Nazis came to power in 1933, as did all other modern art movements, which the Nazis officially characterised as "degenerate". Many important examples of German Expressionist art were destroyed and the artists obliged to cease painting or go into exile.

**569. George Grosz**
*Metropolis, 1916-17*

Oil on canvas. 100 x 102 cm

# GROUND FLOOR

The changes which took place in the visual arts in the early years of the twentieth century were probably the most radical in the entire history of art. While the term "avant-garde" is sometimes used in a general way to refer to any type of artistic innovation, generally those associated with modern art, it is best applied to those movements which took place between around 1907 (the beginning of the lead-up to Cubism) and 1924 (the publication of the First Surrealist Manifesto). The main characteristics of avant-garde art at this time were: 1. A desire to break with existing art movements, particularly with immediately preceding avant-garde movements; 2. The belief that art, like language, depended on a fixed set of rules, and that the most profound artistic innovations came about by replacing one set of rules with another; 3. A faith in the progress of history; 4. As a consequence of all the above, a willingness to consider the work of art as, a. an example of a new set of rules which would be presented in a polemical manner; b. an action which announced future intentions, and an experiment similar to a scientific breakthrough.

As the notion of the avant-garde, defined as above, took hold in modern art, these principles were to the fore. Once the notion of modernity had been established, the polemical spirit which subordinated the work of art to the doctrinal principles of the avant-garde lost ground in favour of an increased emphasis on the individual work. Some artists, such as Picasso, abandoned the experimental avant-garde at a relatively early date, around 1913 or 1914, other artists did so later. In general it can be said that the experimental avant-garde split away from the mainstream of modern art in the late 1920s and was completely marginalised after World War II.

The most important avant-garde movements in the period prior to World War I are Cubism and Futurism.

Cubism sprang from the collaboration between Pablo Ruiz Picasso (1881-1973) and Georges Braque (1882-1963) between 1908 and 1914. Initially limited to the work of just these two painters, it spread in Paris artistic circles from 1910 onwards. If the Impressionist, Post-Impressionist and Fauve artists dedicated themselves to capturing the fleeting moment, impressions and moods, with an emphasis on light and colour, then Picasso and Braque, taking Cézanne as their starting point, concentrated on volume and space. *Still-life with Glasses and Fruits* (cat. 708) and *The Park at*

710. **Pablo Picasso**
*Man with a Clarinet, 1911-12*

Oil on canvas. 106 x 69 cm

## The Experimental Avant-gardes

*Carrières-Saint-Denis* (cat. 479) belong to the early phase. If we compare these two paintings with *Woman with a Mandolin* (cat. 478) and *Man with a Clarinet* (cat. 710) we will understand the process which culminated in fully-developed Cubism. The first stage of this process is a reduction of the shapes of objects into geometrically simple volumes. This is followed by a sort of flattening of the volumes within the picture plane, as if they were being viewed from two points of view at once, combined with a rhythmic structuring of the picture surface. To reinforce the rhythmic effect the points of view are multiplied and the volumes painted as increasingly incomplete and open, to the point where they appear to be dissolving in the space around them. Finally, all that is left of these forms are a few lines or schematic symbols distributed across a network of small facets like cut glass. The vibration of light across this network creates spatial depth and the impression of the forms which occupy it.

Having arrived this far, Cubism seemed to be heading towards total abstraction. The most eloquent spokesman for this approach was Piet Mondrian (1872-1944), as can be seen in his *Composition in grey/blue* (cat. 678). Braque and Picasso chose another path. For them abstract art belonged to the nineteenth century in that it could only express states of mind. In looking for a new artistic sensibility which suited the modern age, they determined to reintroduce the physical appearance of objects into their work. The first step was to develop a centripetal composition which enabled them to emphasise the presence of objects. Next they introduced varied colours and textures. Finally they abandoned the all-over surface to create a new type of spatial depth built up through the juxtaposition of contrasting planes in the manner of a collage. Picasso's *Head of a Man* (cat. 707) illustrates the Cubist style of this period, known as Synthetic Cubism. For Picasso and Braque it was actually a way out of Cubism and a rejection of rules which took them towards a post-avant-garde position.

The Cubism of Juan Gris (1887-1927) followed its own path. During the second decade of the century he used a compositional structure that was basically derived from Analytical Cubism but with colour playing a key role, as in *The Smoker* (cat. 567).

The art historian Douglas Cooper grouped the art of Léger together with that of Gris, Braque and Picasso, calling it "Essential Cubism", in order to distinguish it from the work of other artists.

**634. Frantisek Kupka**

*Positionings of Mobile Graphic Elements I, 1912-13*

Oil on canvas. 200 x 194 cm

Nonetheless, Léger's method of deconstructing forms is closer to the study of movement in the art of Delaunay and the Futurists, than to Picasso's and Braque's understanding of volumes. *The Staircase (Second State)* (cat. 645) belongs to a group of works from 1913 and 1914 which have the general title "Contrasts of Forms", and represent the culmination of Léger's version of Cubism.

Futurism was an Italian movement of a mainly literary nature, founded in 1909 by Filippo Maria Marinetti. Its main doctrine was an exaltation of speed, of the future and (at least to begin with) of

# The Experimental
Avant-gardes

war. The *Technical Manifesto of Futurist Painting* was published in 1910. *Patriotic Demonstration* (cat. 459) by Giacomo Balla (1871-1958) illustrates one of Futurism's characteristics. Balla represents the waving of the flags and the movement of the crowds of demonstrators as a rhythmical overlay of curving forms which recall Art Nouveau. Another tendency in Futurist painting is evident in the work of Gino Severini (1883-1966), an artist who moved to Paris in 1896 and developed stylistically from Neo-impressionism to Cubism in parallel with the Duchamp brothers, Delaunay and Kupka. *Expansion of Light* (cat. 752), a luminous space painted in a pointillist technique, dilates in a series of rhythmic dance movements. The painting is a high point of pre-war Futurist art.

645. **Fernand Léger**
*The Staircase (Second State), 1914*

Oil on canvas. 88 x 124.5 cm

715. **Liubov Popova**
*Still-life with Instruments, 1915*
Oil on canvas. 105.5 x 69.2 cm

Most of the artistic innovations of the second decade of the century can be understood as combinations of: a. the Cubist method of deconstructing forms; b. The Futurist method of representing movement; c. the search for a new approach to colour derived from Neo-impressionism. The possibilities which these approaches held for painting are evident in the *The Parisian Woman* (cat. 517) by Robert Delaunay, and in *Simultaneous Contrasts* (cat. 518) by his wife Sonia Terk.

It was the poet Guillaume Apollinaire who invented the term "Orphic Cubism" for the painting of Robert and Sonia Delaunay. He included other artists in this movement including the Czech painter Frantisek Kupka (1871-1957). The Delaunays and Kupka experimented with abstract painting from 1910, at the same time as Kandinsky in Munich. This was not a coincidence: it stems from

## The Experimental
## Avant-gardes

a widely-held idea in Europe in the late nineteenth century that there were profound connections between the different forms of artistic expression, particularly between painting and music. *Study for the Language of the Verticals* (cat. 790) exploits this idea directly, almost naively. Kupka's painting was enriched by his association with the Orphic movement, as can be seen in his *Positionings of Mobile Graphic Elements I* (cat. 634), an early masterpiece.

Mijail Larionov (1881-1964) defined Rayonism as a synthesis of Cubism, Futurism and Orphism. He founded Rayonism in Moscow in 1913 together with Natalia Gontcharova (1881-1962). *Street with Lights* (cat. 636) was painted prior to this, but it heralds the new style. The best example of its mature form in the museum is *Rayonist Landscape* by Natalia Gontcharova (cat. 562).

Within the context of the Russian avant-garde of the period 1910-1920, no artist better understood Cubism than Liubov Popova (1889-1924). *Still-life with Instruments* (cat. 715) is a key painting for understanding her development towards abstraction under the influence of Malevich, another Russian painter influenced by Cubism. The two paintings by Popova entitled *Painterly Architectonic* and *Architectonic Composition* (cats. 714 and 716) belong to a series of almost completely abstract works painted between 1916 and 1918.

The Russian Revolution heralded the beginning of a propitious period for Russian artists. The break with the past, the emphatic commitment to the future and the spirit of experimentation were attitudes to be found in all sectors of society. The main trends within the Russian revolutionary avant-garde were Suprematism and Constructivism. Kasimir Malevich was the leader of the Suprematist movement. In addition to Popova's *Painterly Architectonics* series mentioned above, other paintings from this movement in the museum include *Composition* (cat. 625) by Ivan Kliun (1873-1943), and *Suprematist Composition* (cat. 506) by Ilya Chashnik (1902-1929), although this last picture is a relatively late work which has stylistic links with Constructivism.

The first leader of the Constructivist movement was the sculptor Tatlin, although the ideas of a number of architects such as the Vesnin brothers were essential to its early development. The movement's central idea was that the work of art need not represent anything, not even geometric forms; on the contrary, it should limit itself to expressing the rules which govern its existence in

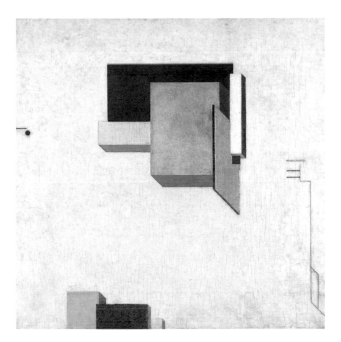

652. **El Lissitzky**
*Proun 1C, 1919*
Oil on cardboard. 68 x 68 cm

675. **László Moholy-Nagy**
*Large Railway Painting, 1920*
Oil on canvas. 100 x 77 cm

# The Experimental
# Avant-gardes

space. One of the consequences of this doctrine is the disappearance of the differences between architecture, painting and sculpture. The works which El Lissitzky (1890-1941) called "Prouns" are a good example of Constructivist theory. In *Proun 1C* (cat. 652), one of the best works from this series, the central arrangement of the figures recalls Malevich. *Proun 4B* (cat. 651) already reveals the dynamic use of space characteristic of Constructivism.

The relationship between the artistic and political avant-garde movements became less cordial in the 1920s and ended in the early 1930s with the disappearance of the avant-garde art scene and the imposition of so-called "Socialist Realism" by the Soviet authorities.

Between 1922 and 1925 Lissitzky worked in Germany and Switzerland. While there his presence contributed to the development of the avant-garde in Central Europe. The most important artists with whom he had contact were László Moholy-Nagy (1895-1946), Kurt Schwitters (1887-1948) and Theo van Doesburg (1883-1931). *Large Railway Painting* (cat. 675) is a key early work by Moholy-Nagy. Following his meeting with Lissitzky the artist was able to develop his own version of Constructivism when in 1923 he joined the Bauhaus, a school of art, architecture and design created with the aim of bringing these three disciplines together. The name of Kurt Schwitters is generally associated with Dada, a movement which started during the war years. Although very active, Dada was not a unified movement and Schwitters was perhaps its most independent member. From 1919 he channelled most of his activity into *collage* (two-dimensional works) and *assemblage* (work incorporating three-dimensional objects). *Merzbild 1A* (cat. 746) is one of his first *assemblages*. While it still shows traces of Expressionism, the assembled pieces function mainly through their visual and tactile qualities. Schwitters developed from this starting point through the 1920s, coming close to Constructivism, as can be seen in his *Eight-sided Composition* (cat. 745).

Theo van Doesburg belonged to the *De Stijl* group, founded in 1917. The group was the principal exponent of the experimental avant-garde in the inter-war period. It called for a reduction of pictorial language to its most basic elements: the primary colours and vertical and horizontal lines. *Pictorial Motif: Still-life* (cat. 526) by Van Doesburg is an important example of this doctrine painted at a time when the artist was closest to Mondrian, the group's guid-

**746. Kurt Schwitters**
*Merzbild 1A (The Psychiatrist), 1919*

Mixed technique and montage on canvas. 48.5 x 38.5 cm

ing spirit and initial inspiration. The work of Piet Mondrian, with its combination of extreme rigour and enormous visual power, have made the artist one of the great myths of the century. In addition to the transitional Cubist work mentioned on page 136, the museum has two other paintings: *Composition I* (cat. 677) is a classic example of the clarity, monumentality and simplicity of his mature style, while *New York City* (cat. 679) is a marvellous hymn to modern life. Started during the war, it remained unfinished on his death.

It would perhaps not be an exaggeration to attribute part of the submerged affinity which exists between the work of Mondrian and the principal current of art history to his association between 1916 and 1918 with Bart van der Leck (1876-1958), a painter from Utrecht who was a founder member of *De Stijl* but left the group in 1918. Few art historians would place Van der Leck among the principal artists of this century, but his *Mountain Landscape in Algeria with a Village* (cat. 641) is one of the most beautiful paintings in these rooms.

**679. Piet Mondrian**
*New York City, New York, 1940-42*

Oil, pencil, charcoal and tape on canvas. 117 x 110 cm

# 45-46 The Synthesis of Modernity in Europe and the United States

In 1932 the art historian Henry Russell Hitchcock and the architect Philip Johnson organised an exhibition on architecture at the Museum of Modern Art (MoMA) in New York devised by the museum's director Alfred H. Barr. Although the works exhibited were from differing movements of avant-garde art, the two men decided to group them all together under the single heading of "The International Style". In the case of painting and sculpture, however, Barr did not set out to find a shared style. Instead, he organised two exhibitions which charted the principal routes which modern art had taken: 1. From Cubism to Abstraction, and 2. Fantastic Art, Dada and Surrealism. During the 1930s there were various initiatives which, like Barr's, were based on a unified vision of modern art. They paved the way for what was to come after World War II, namely the organisation of large group exhibitions, the creation of specialised publications and museums, and its appearance as a subject in universities and art schools. These were all stages in the rise of syncretic and post-avant-garde modern art to its position of dominance which culminated around 1960.

These external pointers towards a process of convergence and synthesis were also evident within the art itself. Some were already evident in the 1920s. One important example is that of "Synthetic Cubism", a stylistic term used from World War I onwards. In contrast to Analytical Cubism, Synthetic Cubism did not involve a new set of rules; it was a way of painting which spread through imitation, analogy or metamorphosis. This absence of rules and its ability to adapt itself to different artistic trends ensured its survival and made it one of the most influential pictorial languages within modern art.

Almost all of the paintings by Georges Braque (1882-1963) made after his return from the war in 1917 could be described as Synthetic Cubism. The pictorial space of *The pink Tablecloth* (cat. 480) is still Cubist in the sense of the term as applied to the artist's collages of 1913 and 1914. At the same time, the biomorphic forms, the monumental composition, the earthy textures and the dull palette point towards what was to become an important artistic trend in the 1940s.

*Composition. The Disk* (cat. 643) is part of a group of works by Fernand Léger (1881-1955) painted after the artist's return from the war which evoke the mechanised confusion of urban life. It is a type of adaptation of Orphic painting of the pre-war period to the

709. **Pablo Picasso**
*Harlequin with a Mirror, 1923*

Oil on canvas. 100 x 81 cm

## The Synthesis of Modernity
## in Europe and the United States

new spatial construction of Synthetic Cubism. In *The Bridge* (cat. A855), painted five years later, we find the same approach to spatial setting, but the picture space evokes a luminous and static world. The difference also marks a change of taste. Léger has joined the ranks of artists who were looking for a new order, and, as the poet André Salmon said in 1920, abandoned Cézanne to follow Seurat.

In a way Picasso was also among this group. The search for calm and order in his work is usually associated with the classicising figuration evident in his art at this time. However, although they sometimes coincide, classicism and a return to order are not necessarily the same thing. His most famous example of Synthetic Cubism, *The three Musicians* of 1921, now in MoMA, reflects the return to order to no less a degree than *Pan's Flute,* a classicising work from 1923. In addition, while the *Harlequin with a Mirror* (cat. 709) is also a classicising painting from the same year, its inspiration is completely different. Only the Harlequin's face has something in common with the gods or classical athletes of *Pan's Flute.* In fact it is a mask. At this period Harlequin represents Picasso himself, an evocation of his trip to Italy and his meeting with Olga (who was to become his wife) six years earlier. The figure looking at itself in the mirror is a metaphor for the passing of time, as in Baroque painting. Stylistically the painting seems like an assemblage of fragments painted by different hands. The areas of white cloth are unrealistically solid while the thick impasto of the colours give the torso a disordered fleshiness. The whole painting gives off an atmosphere of bitter melancholy.

That same year André Breton published an article in which he attacked Cubism but "saluted in the work of Picasso the first signs of a tendency to *illegality* in modern art". This rejection of rules and codes would have a twofold effect on the development of Surrealism: it would guarantee its influence over a period of twenty years, and at the same time it would allow for a certain ambiguity as to who was affiliated with it. Some important artists who were not part of the movement, such as Picasso, could be claimed as belonging to it; others generally considered Surrealists, such as Ernst and Miró, could distance themselves from it for long periods while they evolved along their own lines.

Max Ernst (1891-1976) internalised the plurality of pictorial languages within Surrealism. The museum has three works by him

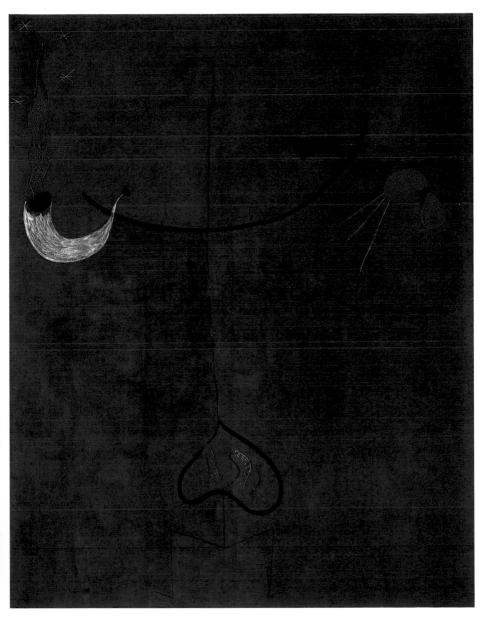

**672. Joan Miró**
*Catalan Peasant with Guitar, 1924*

Oil on canvas. 147 x 114 cm

## The Synthesis of Modernity
## in Europe and the United States

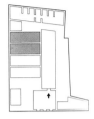

which are all completely different from each other. *Untitled* (cat. 538) and *33 Girls looking for the white Butterfly* (cat. 537) are on show in room 45. *Single and conjugal Trees* (cat. 535) is on show in room 47.

One of the fundamental principles of Surrealism is psychic automatism, a method which relies on the elimination of all rational control in the process of creation. In the field of poetry this results in a form of writing based on the free association of words. With painting it is formed by the spontaneous association of visual images, as in a dream. There are two ways to achieve this: using a conventional technique, as with Dalí's "photographic" technique (see room 47), or through an "automatic" technique based on spontaneity. Joan Miró (1893-1983) was the chief exponent of this second approach. *Catalan Peasant with Guitar* (cat. .672) is one of a group of five works which illustrate the key moment in his development as a Surrealist artist. *The Lightning Bird blinded by the Fire of the Moon* (cat. 674) is a beautiful miniature whose pictorial language reminds us of the "Constellations" series of 1939 to 1941.

In the MoMA exhibition which we discussed above, Alfred Barr presented Dadaism and Surrealism within the context of a tradition of fantasy which stretched back to the Middle Ages, and included Klee, Kandinsky and Chagall among its followers. Born in Russia, Marc Chagall (1887-1985) moved to Paris in 1910 and came into contact with Léger and the Orphist group. In *The grey House* (cat. 500), painted soon after his return to Russia in 1914, the influence of the Paris avant-garde artists is still obvious. *The Rooster* (cat. 499) and *The Madonna of the Village* (cat. 497) are characteristic of the style which he developed after his permanent return to France in 1922. His painting was expressive, poetic and filled with colours based on the Russian Jewish folk-culture of his youth.

Wassily Kandinsky (1866-1944) and Paul Klee (1879-1940) both belonged to the Munich group *The Blue Rider* (see room 38). Taking its point of departure from German Expressionist landscape painting, Kandinsky's art developed through a series of transitional phases, reaching what he called abstract painting in 1910-1911. Through pure colour devoid of figurative references Kandinsky was searching for that power to set loose images and feelings normally achieved by music. Its effect can be seen in *Painting with three Spots* (cat. 609). Despite biographical similarities, Kandinsky and

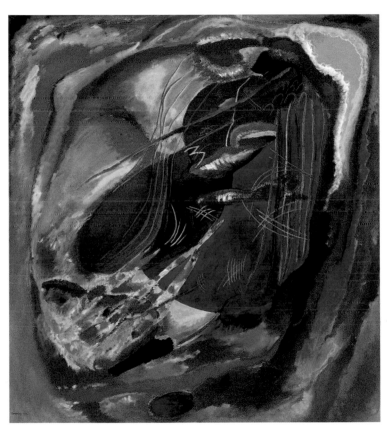

609. **Wassily Kandinsky**
*Painting with three Spots no. 196, 1914*

Oil on canvas. 121 x 111 cm

Klee represent two contrasting artistic personalities. The analogy between art and music was important for both of them, but in very different ways; in music Klee looked less for a torrent of sensations as for its synthetic character or game-like structure. *Revolving House* (cat. 624) is like a lesson in descriptive geometry which culminates in ecstasy. *Omega 5 (Dummy)* (cat. 623) is part of the Gothic grotesque tradition, which for Klee fulfilled a similar role to that of the Mediterranean classical world for Picasso.

## The Synthesis of Modernity
## in Europe and the United States

Neither Klee nor Kandinsky lived to see the end of the war. Among the consequences that this had for modern art it is worth mentioning two that would probably have surprised both artists: modern art came out on the winning side and New York became the principal venue for innovative art in the second half of the century. The most important of the new movements after the war was known as "Informalism" in Europe and "Abstract Expressionism" in the United States. Two precedents are usually cited for Abstract Expressionism: the Cubist construction of space and Surrealist automatism. The first was well known in the US in the 1930s. While Surrealism was initially less known this changed when a large part of the Paris group of Surrealist artists emigrated to New York in 1939 at the start of the war. Arshile Gorky (1905-1948), an artist who had followed Picasso's work very closely in the 1930s, was one of the first American artists to take up Surrealist automatism. *Hugging* (cat. 563) has a spatial construction based on the Cubist

563. **Arshile Gorky**
*Hugging, 1945*

Oil on canvas. 64.7 x 82.7 cm

713. **Jackson Pollock**
*Brown and Silver I, c. 1951*

Enamel and silver paint on canvas. 145 x 101 cm

# The Synthesis of Modernity
# in Europe and the United States

approach which Gorky has transformed through a series of expressive distortions, onto which he has superimposed a floating colour derived from Miró. *Last Painting* (cat. 564) reveals a third element: the German Expressionist tradition. The influence of German Expressionism is more easily seen in the work of Willem de Kooning (1904-1997). In his important early work *Abstraction* (cat. 630), a furious wind of colour tears apart the scaffolding of the post-Cubist space. *Red Man with Moustache* (cat. 631) has a red and green palette which recalls that used by the *Die Brücke* artists in 1907. The Cubist space has disappeared, leaving only a non-figurative and purely optic space which takes form through the free play of the brushstrokes on the canvas.

This new type of space is certainly the most important development within post-war art. *Brown and Silver I* (cat. 713) by Jackson Pollock (1912-1956) is a classic example of the method which led to its discovery: taking Surrealist automatism to its ultimate consequences, applying it to the brushwork, the stroke or the gesture with which the colour is applied to the canvas. However the same effect was reached by other methods. *Green on Maroon* (cat. 729) by Mark Rothko (1903-1970) and *Earth Rhythms* (cat. 771) by Mark Tobey (1890-1976) also use the non-representative space which we saw in the work of Pollock. While these two works are painted in very different ways, one by superimposing broad transparent glazes, the other by building up a succession of brushmarks, in both cases the pulsating vibration of the pictorial space depends entirely on colour.

European artists also achieved a similar type of pictorial space. To define it, it may help to recall the precedents suggested by Rosenblum (see room 31): the luminous and total space in which Malevich and Kliun floated their figures (see room 43), and ultimately the space which silhouettes Friedrich's horizons. *Venice was all gold* (cat. 547; hanging in the central atrium) by Lucio Fontana (1899-1968) could even hint at more distant roots in the art of Byzantine Venice.

729. **Mark Rothko**
*Green on Maroon, 1961*
Mixed media on canvas. 258 x 229 cm

# 47-48 Late Surrealism, the Figurative Tradition and Pop Art

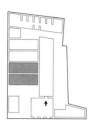

The process of synthesis described in the last chapter ended in the early 1960s as modern art came to be generally accepted. Even though the period which followed is still very close to our own time, we can confidently say that the dominant tendency which emerged was that of Pop Art. The museum has a small group of very high quality works which represent this movement. Hanging with them are works which represent other pictorial trends of lesser importance in relation to the dominant style of Pop Art.

The most important of these other trends is derived from Surrealism. In the previous chapter we discussed the Surrealist practice of spontaneously associating images, as in dreams, represented through a traditional pictorial language. The artist who best illustrates this form of Surrealism is Salvador Dalí (1904-1989). His *Dream caused by the Flight of a Bee around a Pomegranate one Second before Awakening* (cat. 510) depicts the artist's wife Gala asleep nude in the middle of a fantasy landscape filled with dream images. In contrast to Dalí's painting, the art of Yves Tanguy (1900-1955) represents a universe filled with unidentifiable people and objects. René Magritte (1898-1967) was one of the founders of the Belgian Surrealist movement. Although his pictorial language is a conventional one like that of Dalí, Magritte was not interested in the sub-conscious; his associations of images reveal conceptual paradoxes. *The Key to the Field* (cat. 657) represents a window looking on to the countryside. The glass is broken and in the fallen pieces of glass we see the same landscape as a painted image: the viewer does not know if the window is transparent or opaque, real or fictional.

Figurative painting survived throughout the entire twentieth century, practised by a wide variety of artists and schools who do not represent a continuous tradition. One of the most notable schools in the United States was Precisionism, a movement which developed in the 1930s and which had something in common with the German New Objectivity. Charles Sheeler (1883-1965), the most well-known of this group, painted *Canyons* (cat. 757), an impersonal representation of the skyscrapers and office blocks to be found in the centre of any North American city.

Ben Shahn (1898-1969) is the most notable American exponent of Social Realism, a movement which sprang from the crisis of 1929 as a response to the resulting economic depres-

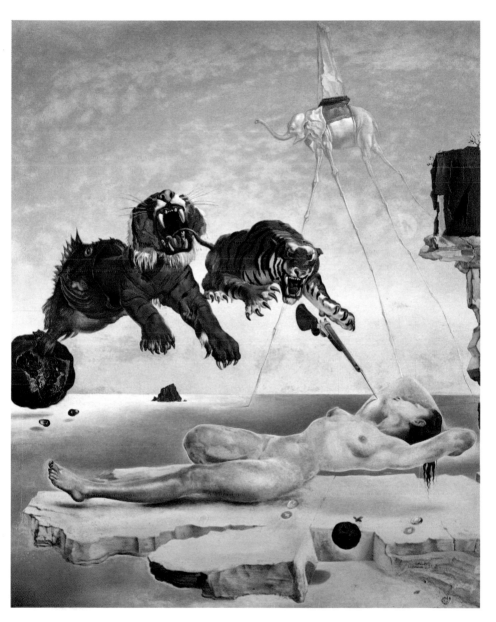

510. **Salvador Dalí**
*Dream caused by the Flight of a Bee around a
Pomegranate one Second before Awakening, 1944*

Oil on cardboard. 51 x 41 cm

157

## Late Surrealism, the Figurative Tradition and Pop Art

sion. Like other politically committed artists of his time, Shahn often worked as an illustrator, which left a permanent mark on his work. *Four-piece Orchestra* (cat. 754) shows three people enjoying a moment of leisure, two of them dressed as workers. In *Carnival* (cat. 756) a man sleeps in a public park far removed from the happiness of the passing couples.

Edward Hopper (1882-1967) is undoubtedly the most important North American Realist painter of the twentieth century. He brought to his work stylistic elements from the history of European painting, from Piero della Francesca to Vermeer. *Girl at a Sewing Machine* (cat. 595) belongs to a series which depict women working in domestic interiors. In *Hotel Room* (cat. 594) the painting is dominated by the figure of the girl seated on the bed and reading what looks like a railway timetable. The electric light within the room makes the night outside even darker.

Balthus (1908) is one of the most well-known European figurative artists. His painting is located on the margins of modernity and aims to recapture the metaphysical atmosphere of fifteenth-century art. *The Card Game* (cat. 460) is an important example of his search for monumentality and of the implicitly erotic atmosphere which characterises his style.

The School of London, formed by Michael Andrews (1928-1996), Leon Kossoff (1926), Frank Auerbach (1931) and Lucian Freud (1922) is possibly the most coherent and important group of figurative painters formed in the second half of the century. While their work is stylistically varied, they share an interest in the human figure and in urban landscapes. They also share a certain expressionist tendency which is rarely made obvious in their paintings. Of these artist the best represented in the museum is Lucian Freud, whose paintings exploit the distortions achieved by adopting unusual viewpoints. *Reflection with two Children* (cat. 550) from 1965 and *Large Interior. Paddington* (cat. 549) perfectly illustrate these characteristics. *Portrait of Baron H.H. Thyssen-Bornemisza* (cat. 551) is set against a background of Watteau's *Pierrot content,* which also belongs to this collection (see room 28).

Francis Bacon (1909-1992) was close to the School of London, although older and more famous than the other artists of the group. His style, which has connections with Surrealism and Expressionism, is far removed from traditional figuration. Bacon's

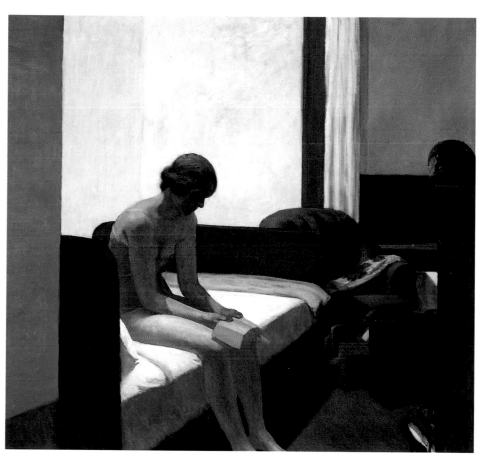

**594. Edward Hopper**
*Hotel Room, 1931*

Oil on canvas. 152.4 x 165.7 cm

paintings frequently depict bare rooms with figures who are isolated and expressively distorted. *Portrait of George Dyer in a Mirror* (cat. 458) depicts a friend who was also the artist's usual model in the 1960s.

The last room in the museum displays a group of works characteristic of Pop Art. This term was first employed by the critic Lawrence Alloway to describe a movement which developed in England in the late 1950s. Its point of departure was an awareness of technological advances and their cultural consequences, especially in the field of communication. The language of Pop Art was characterised by the presence of images taken from advertising, comics and the mass media. However, Pop Art did more than invent a new iconography: it was equivalent to a rethinking of modernity, a rethinking as profound as that of the arrival of the early Baroque after the Renaissance and Mannerism (see room 12). In contrast to the features which characterise modern art at its developed stage, Pop Art: 1. is extrovert and aims to make the work of art objective and impersonal; 2. gives

460. **Balthus**
*The Card Game, 1948-50*

Oil on canvas. 140 x 194 cm

**458. Francis Bacon**
*Portrait of George Dyer in a Mirror, 1968*

Oil on canvas. 198 x 147 cm

## Late Surrealism, the Figurative
## Tradition and Pop Art

priority to symbolic, allegorical or literary associations; 3. makes use of pre-existing visual and cultural material.

This change of direction is evident in the career of the painter Robert Rauschenberg (1925). As a young artist he was associated with Abstract Expressionism, and throughout his artistic life Rauschenberg remained faithful to certain principles characteristic of traditional modernism, such as psychic automatism. *Express* (cat. 721) was painted at the time when the artist won the International Painting prize at the Venice Biennale, an event which greatly helped to promote Pop Art on the international scene.

Among the stylistic precedents to Pop Art is the free association of images practised by the Dada artists, particularly Schwitters (see room 43). This Dadaist tradition was kept alive in the United States in the 1940s and 1950s in the work of artists such as Joseph Cornell (1903-1972). In the late 1950s art critics detected a neo-Dadaist tendency among certain artists including Rauschenberg. However, the original Dadaism was an essentially introspective attitude in which the artist reflected on the nature of modern art. By contrast, for the Pop artist modern art was already a given fact, and so the artist asked himself or herself questions about the nature of the age in which he or she was living. As a consequence, Pop Art involved a sort of ideological Futurism, taking its place in an artistic tradition which had glorified the mechanical and impersonal aspect of modern life throughout the twentieth century. Léger's late painting, and in the US those of Stuart Davis (1894-1964) are examples of this confidence in the future of technology. The two works by Davis in room 48, in particular the later one, *Pochade* (cat. 514) are visual proof of this hypothesis. While Stuart Davis is a good example of an artist whose career starts from the synthesis of modernity and develops towards a Pop sensibility, Richard Lindner (1901-1978) illustrates another trajectory. German by birth and a graphic artist by training, Lindner experienced the last years of Expressionism and New Objectivity at close hand in Germany in the 1930s. This experience and the influence of Léger contributed to the formation of his personal vision of North American culture.

Along with the various paths which lead to Pop Art we should mention those which travel away from it. Ronald B. Kitaj (1932) and David Hockney (1937) form part of the London group

721. **Robert Rauschenberg**
*Express, 1963*
Oil on canvas with screenprint, 183 x 305 cm

which originally inspired the term "Pop Art". However, both artists avoided using its characteristic iconography and developed towards a figurative painting which was by nature narrative, and in the case of Kitaj, densely literary and reflective.

Despite its stylistic variety, the feature for which Pop Art undoubtedly became best known was its use of mass media iconography. A key element in setting up this historical association was the international attention generated by a series of paintings made by Roy Lichtenstein (1923-1997) from 1962. In 1963 the artist stated that in painting episodes from comics the only thing that interested him –just like Ingres when he painted his portraits– was line and colour. *Woman in the Bath* (cat. 648) is one of the most beautiful of these paintings from Lichtenstein's classic period. The fact that we can admire this painting in terms of line and colour (as with the art of Mondrian, Léger, Picasso or Matisse) is paradoxical. We recognise a masterpiece by its historical significance, its ability to imprint onto the art of its own

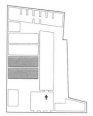

time a new and different direction to that taken by masterpieces of the past. At the same time we recognise it as a masterpiece because it invites admiration, along with other great works of art, in a timeless context. The realisation that these two apparently contradictory ways of appreciating a great work of art are in fact one and the same is the key to aesthetic experience and the *raison d'être* of the history of art and of museums.

514. **Stuart Davis**
*Pochade, 1958*

Oil on canvas. 130 x 152 cm

**648. Roy Lichtenstein**
*Woman in the Bath, 1963*

Oil on canvas. 171 x 171 cm

# LIST OF WORKS

## ITALIAN PRIMITIVES
## ROOM 1

424.a-c. ANONYMOUS VENETIAN around 1300-1310. *Triptych with the Virgin and Child.* Tempera on panel, central panel: 80 x 102 cm; wings: 76 .8 x 25.5 cm.

257. ANONYMOUS VENETIAN around 1360. *The Virgin of Humility with Angels and a Donor,* c. 1360. Tempera on panel, 68.8 x 56.7 cm.

70. BARTOLOMEO DI MESSER BULGARINO. *The Virgin and Child enthroned between four Angels, a Martyr and Saint John the Baptist,* c. 1340-1345. Tempera on panel, 48 x 26 cm.

123. DADDI, Bernardo. *The Crucifixion,* c. 1330-1335. Tempera on panel, 37.4 x 22.2 cm.

133. DUCCIO DI BUONINSEGNA. *Christ and the Woman of Samaria,* 1310-1311. Tempera and gold on panel, 43.5 x 46 cm.

151. GADDI, Agnolo. *The Crucifixion,* c. 1390. Tempera on panel, 32.5 x 30.3 cm.

161. GIOVANNI DI PAOLO. *The Virgin of Humility,* c. 1440. Tempera on panel, 32.5 x 22.5 cm.

162. GIOVANNI DI PAOLO. *Saint Catherine before the Pope in Avignon,* c. 1460. Tempera on panel, 29 x 29 cm.

228.a-c. LORENZO VENEZIANO. *Portable triptych with The Crucifixion,* c. 1370-1375. Tempera on panel, central panel: 83.6 x 30.7 cm; wings: 83 x 15 cm.

231. LUCA DI TOMMÈ. *The Adoration of the Magi,* c. 1360-1365. Tempera on panel, 41 x 42 cm.

247. MASTER OF 1355. *The Coronation of the Virgin with five Angels,* 1355. Tempera and gold on panel, 86 x 52.5 cm.

256. MASTER OF THE MAGDALEN. *The Virgin and Child enthroned with Saint Dominic, Saint Martin and two Angels,* c. 1290. Tempera and panel, 177 x 86.5 cm.

260. MASTER OF THE POMPOSA CHAPTER-HOUSE. *The Crucifixion,* c. 1320. Tempera on panel, 29 x 20.5 cm.

412. UGOLINO DI NERIO. *The Crucifixion with the Virgin, Saint John and Angels,* c. 1330-1335. Tempera on panel, 135 x 95.5 cm.

425. VITALE DA BOLOGNA. *The Crucifixion* c. 1335. Tempera on panel, 93 x 51.2 cm.

## GOTHIC PAINTING
## ROOM 2

272. ANONYMOUS GERMAN active in Westphalia. *The Virgin and Child in the Garden,* c. 1410. Panel, 28.6 x 18.5 cm.

273. ANONYMOUS GERMAN active in Westphalia. *Christ on the Cross as Salvator Mundi,* c. 1410. Panel, 28.5 x 18.5 cm.

245.a-c. ANONYMOUS GERMAN active in Cologne. *Annunciation Triptych,* Mixed media on panel, central panel: 34.3 x 16.5 cm; wings: 34.3 x 8.5 cm.

268.a. ANONYMOUS GERMAN, around 1420. *The Descent from the Cross,* c. 1420. Oil on panel, 62 x 30 cm.

44.a-e. MASTER BERTRAM. *Triptych of the Holy Face of Christ,* 1395-1410. Oil on panel, central panel: 30.8 x 24.2 cm; wings: 30.8 x 12 cm.

199. HUGUET, Jaume (Circle of). *The Pilgrims' Mass.* Tempera and gold on panel, 83 x 72 cm.

210. KOERBECKE, Johann. *The Assumption of the Virgin,* just before 1457. Oil on panel, 93.1 x 64.2 cm.

233. MAELESSKIRCHER, Gabriel. *Saint Luke the Evangelist,* 1478. Oil on panel, 77 x 32.2 cm.

234. MAELESSKIRCHER, Gabriel. *Saint Matthew the Evangelist,* 1478. Oil on panel, 77.4 x 32.2 cm.

235. MAELESSKIRCHER, Gabriel. *Saint John the Evangelist,* 1478. Oil on panel, 77.2 x 32 cm.

236. MAELESSKIRCHER, Gabriel. *Saint Mark the Evangelist,* 1478. Oil on panel, 77.1 x 32.2 cm.

237. MAELESSKIRCHER, Gabriel. *Saint Luke painting the Virgin,* 1478. Oil on panel, 77 x 32 cm.

238. MAELESSKIRCHER, Gabriel. *The Miracle of Saint Matthew taming the Dragon,* 1478. Oil on panel, 77.2 x 32.2 cm.

239. MAELESSKIRCHER, Gabriel. *The Miracle of the Host at the Tomb of Saint John the Evangelist,* 1478. Oil on panel, 77 x 32 cm.

240. MAELESSKIRCHER, Gabriel. *The Martyrdom of Saint Mark*, 1478. Oil on panel, 77.2 x 32.2 cm.

246. MASTER OF THE VISION OF SAINT JOHN. *Saints Cosmas, Damian and Pantaleon*, c. 1455. Oil on panel, 130.5 x 72.2 cm.

282. MATES, Joan. *Saint John the Baptist and Saint John the Evangelist with a Donor* c. 1410. Oil on panel, 191 x 121 cm.

## EARLY NETHERLANDISH PAINTING ROOM 3

60 BOUTS, Dieric (Follower of). *The Virgin and Child*, c. 1465. Oil on panel, 28.5 x 20 cm.

121. CHRISTUS, Petrus. *The Virgin of the dry Tree*, c. 1450. Oil on panel, 17.4 x 12.4 cm.

124. DARET, Jacques. *The Adoration of the Christ Child*, 1434-1435. Oil on panel, 59.5 x 53 cm.

125. DAVID, Gerard. *The Crucifixion*. Oil on panel, 88 x 56 cm.

137.a-b EYCK, Jan van. *The Annunciation Diptych*, c. 1435-1441. Oil on panel, each wing: 38.8 x 23.2 cm.

142. FLANDES, Juan de. *The Lamentation*, c. 1500. Oil on panel, 23 x 30 cm.

251.a. MASTER OF THE MAGDALEN LEGEND (Attributed to). *Portrait of a Man as Saint Andrew*, c. 1480. Oil on panel, 28.2 x 19.7 cm.

252.a-e. MASTER OF THE SAINT LUCY LEGEND. *Triptych with the Lamentation*, c. 1475. Oil on panel, central panel: 75 x 61 cm; wings: 75 x 27 cm.

253. MASTER OF THE LEGEND OF SAINT URSULA. *The Virgin and Child with two Angels*, c. 1480. Oil on panel, 36.6 x 27 cm.

255. MASTER OF THE ANDRÉ MADONNA. *The Virgin and Child with Angels*, c. 1500. Oil on panel, 62 x 32 cm.

269. MASTER OF THE VIRGO INTER VIRGINES. *The Crucifixion*, c. 1487. Oil on panel, 78 x 58.5 cm.

270. MASTER OF THE VIRGO INTER VIRGINES (Follower of). *The Last Supper*. Oil on panel, 69.7 x 38 cm.

261. MASTER OF THE VIEW OF SAINT GUDULA. *Clothing the Naked*, c. 1470. Oil on panel, 63.5 x 41.5 cm.

435. WEYDEN, Roger van der. *The Virgin and Child enthroned*, c. 1433. Oil on panel, 14.2 x 10.2 cm.

## 15TH-CENTURY ITALIAN PAINTING ROOM 4

94. ANONYMOUS FRANCO-FLEMISH active in Naples. *The Crucifixion*. Tempera on panel, 44.8 x 34 cm.

53. BONIFIGLIO, Benedetto. *The Annunciation*, c. 1455. Gold and tempera on panel, 51 x 36.5 cm.

57. BOTTICINI, Francesco. *Saint Cecilia with Saints Valerian, Tiburtius and a female Donor*. Panel, 52 x 44.5 cm.

61. BRAMANTINO. *The Risen Christ*. Oil on panel, 109 x 73 cm.

107. COSTA, Lorenzo. *The Virgin and Child enthroned*, c. 1495. Oil on panel, 49.5 x 36.5 cm.

168. GOZZOLI, Benozzo. *Saint Jerome with a Saint*, c. 1470. Tempera on panel, 22.3 x 43.5 cm.

344. ROBERTI, Ercole de'. *The Argonauts leaving Colchis*, c. 1480. Panel, 35 x 26.5 cm.

410. TURA, Cosimo. *Saint John the Evangelist on Patmos*, c. 1470. Tempera on panel, 27 x 32 cm.

411. UCCELLO, Paolo. *The Crucifixion with the Virgin, Saint John the Baptist, Saint John the Evangelist and Saint Francis*, c. 1460-1465. Tempera on panel, 45 x 67 cm.

426. VIVARINI, Alvise. *Saint John the Baptist*, c. 1475. Tempera and oil on panel, 48.5 x 33.5 cm.

446. ZOPPO, Marco. *Saint Jerome in the Desert*, 1460-1470. Mixed media on panel, 39 x 29 cm.

## EARLY RENAISSANCE PORTRAITS ROOM 5

11. ANONYMOUS FRANCO-FLEMISH, fifteenth-century. *Posthumous Portrait of Wenceslaus of Luxembourg, Duke of Brabant*, c. 1405-1415. Oil on panel, 34.4 x 25.4 cm.

18. ANTONELLO DA MESSINA. *Portrait of a Man*, c. 1475-1476. Oil on panel, 27.5 x 21 cm.

74. CAMPIN, Robert. *Portrait of a thick-set Man (Robert de Masmines?)*, c. 1425(?). Oil on panel, 35.4 x 23.7 cm.

89. CLEVE, Joos van. *Self-portrait*, c. 1519. Oil on panel, 38 x 27 cm.

105. COSSA, Francesco del. *Portrait of a Man*, 1472-1477. Oil on panel, 38.3 x 27.3 cm.

130. DOMENICO VENEZIANO. *Monk with a Cross,* 1445-1448. Panel, 69 x 44 cm.

141. FLANDES, Juan de. *Portrait of an Infanta (Catherine of Aragon?),* c. 1496. Oil on panel, 31.5 x 21.7 cm.

158. GHIRLANDAIO, Domenico. *Portrait of Giovanna Tornabuoni,* 1488. Mixed media on panel, 77 x 49 cm.

191. HOLBEIN, Hans the Younger. *Portrait of Henry VIII of England,* c. 1534-1536. Oil on panel, 28 x 20 cm.

284.a-b. MEMLING, Hans (a) *Portrait of a young Man praying,* (b) *Vase of Flowers,* c. 1485. Oil on panel, 29.2 x 22.5 cm.

319. PIERO DELLA FRANCESCA. *Portrait of a Boy (Guidobaldo de Montefeltro?),* c. 1483. Tempera on panel, 41 x 27.5 cm.

372. SOLARIO, Andrea. *Portrait of a young Man,* after 1490. Oil on panel, 29.5 x 26 cm.

436. WEYDEN, Roger van der (Attributed to). *Portrait of a Man, (Pierre de Beffrement, Count of Charny?),* c. 1464. Oil on panel, 32 x 22.8 cm.

### THE GALERÍA VILLAHERMOSA ROOM 6

4. AMBERGER, Christoph. *Portrait of Matthäus Schwarz,* 1542. Oil on panel, 73.5 x 61 cm.

188. ANONYMOUS GERMAN around 1525-1530. *Portrait of a young Man ,* c. 1525-1530. Oil on panel 32 x 26 cm.

30. BARTOLOMEO VENETO. *Portrait of a Man,* 1525-1530. Oil on panel, 87.3 x 59 cm.

52. BOLTRAFFIO, Giovanni Antonio. *Portrait of a Lady as Saint Lucy,* c. 1500. Oil on panel, 51.5 x 36.5 cm.

55. BORDONE, Paris. *Portrait of a young Lady,* c. 1540-1560. Oil on canvas, 103 x 83 cm.

64. BRONZINO. *Portrait of a young Man as Saint Sebastian,* c. 1525-1528. Oil on panel, 87 x 76.5 cm.

92. CLOUET, François. *The Love Letter,* c. 1570. Oil on paper laid down on panel, 41.4 x 55 cm.

102. CORREGGIO, Antonio. *Portrait of a Scholar,* c. 1525. Oil on canvas, 55 x 40 cm.

159. GHIRLANDAIO, Ridolfo. *Portrait of a Nobleman of the Capponi Family.* Oil on panel, 80 x 60.5 cm.

230. LOTTO, Lorenzo. *Self-portrait.* Oil on panel, 43 x 35 cm.

330. RAPHAEL. *Portrait of a young Man (Alessandro de Medici?),* c. 1515. Oil on panel, 44 x 29.4 cm.

363. SALINI, Tommaso. *Peasant Boy with a Flask,* c. 1610. Oil on canvas, 99 x 73 cm.

400. TINTORETTO. *Portrait of a Senator,* c. 1580. Oil on canvas, 64 x 49.5 cm.

423. VERONESE, Paolo. *Portrait of a Woman with a Dog,* 1560-1570. Oil on canvas, 105 x 79 cm.

### 16TH-CENTURY ITALIAN PAINTING ROOM 7

29. BARTOLOMMEO, Fra. *The Holy Family with Saint John the Baptist,* c. 1506-1507. Oil on panel, 62 x 47 cm.

33. BECCAFUMI, Domenico. *The Virgin and Child with Saint John and Saint Jerome,* c. 1523-1524. Oil on panel, tondo 85.5 cm diameter.

38. BELLINI, Gentile. *The Annunciation,* c. 1465. Tempera and oil on panel, 133 x 124 cm.

39. BELLINI, Giovanni. *Sacra Conversazione ("Nunc dimittis..."),* 1505-1510. Oil on panel, 62 x 82.5 cm.

63. BRONZINO. *Cosimo I de' Medici in Armour.* Oil on panel, 76.5 x 59 cm.

82. CARPACCIO, Vittore. *Young Knight in a Landscape,* 1510. Oil on canvas, 218.5 x 151.5 cm.

145. FOSCHI, Pierfrancesco di Jacopo. *Portrait of a Lady,* 1530-1535. Oil on panel, 101 x 79 cm.

232. LUINI, Bernardino. *The Virgin and Child with the Infant Saint John the Baptist,* 1523-1525. Oil on canvas, 86 x 60 cm.

309. PALMA VECCHIO. *Sacra Conversazione,* 1515-1520. Oil on canvas, 105 x 136 cm.

310. PALMA VECCHIO. *Portrait of a young Woman, "La Bella",* c. 1525. Oil on canvas, 95 x 80 cm.

320. PIERO DI COSIMO. *The Virgin and Child with Angels,* 1500-1510. Panel, tondo 78 cm diameter.

369. SEBASTIANO DEL PIOMBO. *Portrait of Ferry Carondelet with his Secretaries,* 1510-1512. Oil on panel, 112.5 x 87 cm.

403. TINTORETTO. *The Paradise,* c. 1583. Oil on canvas, 164 x 492 cm. *On show in the central atrium.

405. TITIAN. *Portrait of Doge Francesco Venier*, 1554-1556. Oil on canvas, 113 x 99 cm.

## 16TH-CENTURY GERMAN PAINTING ROOM 8

259. ANONYMOUS GERMAN active in Düren. *Four Scenes from the Passion*, c. 1495-1500. Oil on panel, 163.8 x 55.5 cm.

262. ANONYMOUS GERMAN around 1430. *The Birth of the Virgin*, c. 1430. Panel, 84.5 x 34.7 cm.

263. ANONYMOUS GERMAN around 1430. *The Presentation in the Temple*, c. 1430. Panel, 84.3 x 35 cm.

264. ANONYMOUS GERMAN around 1480. *Portrait of a Woman*, c. 1480. Oil on panel, 50.4 x 39.2 cm.

265. ANONYMOUS GERMAN around 1480. *Portrait of a Man*, c. 1480. Oil on panel, 55 x 43.5 cm.

22. BAEGERT, Derick. *The Good Centurion*, 1477-1478. Oil on panel, 81.5 x 51 cm.

23. BAEGERT, Derick. *Saint Veronica with the Holy Veil and a group of Knights*, 1477-1478. Oil on panel, 113 x 97.5 cm.

24. BAEGERT, Derick. *Christ bearing the Cross*, 1477-1478. Oil on panel, 87 x 98 cm.

25. BAEGERT, Derick. *The kneeling Magdalen*, 1477-1478. Oil on panel, 80 x 42.3 cm.

26. BAEGERT, Derick. *Men playing Dice for Christ's Robe*, 1477-1478. Oil on panel, 159 x 92.3 cm.

67. BRUYN, Barthel The Elder. *Portrait of a Man from the Weinsberg family*, c. 1538-1539. Oil on panel, 35 x 25.5 cm.

68. BRUYN, Barthel The Elder. *Portrait of a Woman*, c. 1538-1539. Oil on panel, 34.9 x 25.5 cm.

69. BRUYN, Barthel The Elder. *The Adoration of the Christ Child*, c. 1520. Oil on panel, 62.5 x 55.5 cm.

71. BURGKMAIR, Hans The Elder. *The Entombment*, c. 1520. Oil on panel, 66.3 x 118.3 cm.

114. CRANACH, Lucas The Elder. *The Virgin and Child with a Bunch of Grapes*, c. 1509-1510. Oil on panel, 71.5 x 44.2 cm.

134. DÜRER, Albrecht. *Christ among the Doctors*, 1506. Oil on panel, 64.3 x 80.3 cm.

212.a-c. KULMBACH, Hans Süss von. *Triptych of the Celestial Rosary*. Oil on panel, central panel: 117 x 84.3 cm, before 1510; wings: 122.5 x 38.5 cm y 122.5 x 37.5 cm, 1513.

250. MASTER OF GROSSGMAIN. *Saint Jerome*, 1498. Oil on panel, 67 x 49 cm.

308. PACHER, Michael (Follower of). *The Virgin and Child with Saint Margaret and Saint Catherine*, c. 1500. Oil on panel, 166 x 76.5 cm.

380. STRIGEL, Bernhard. *The Annunciation to Saint Anna and Saint Joachim*, c. 1505-1510. Oil on panel, 58 x 30 cm.

382. STRÜB, Jakob or Hans. *The Visitation*, c. 1505. Oil on panel, 80 x 54.7 cm.

## ROOM 9

2. ALTDORFER, Albrecht. *Portrait of a Woman*, 1522 (?). Oil on panel, 59 x 45 cm.

258. ANONYMOUS GERMAN School of Lucas Cranach The Elder. *Portrait of a Woman aged 26*, 1525. Oil on panel, 61.6 x 38.8 cm.

54. ANONYMOUS GERMAN around 1490. *Portrait of a Woman wearing the Order of the Swan*, c. 1490. Oil on panel, 44.7 x 28.2 cm.

27. BALDUNG GRIEN, Hans. *Adam and Eve*, 1531. Oil on panel, 147.5 x 67.3 cm.

28. BALDUNG GRIEN, Hans. *Portrait of a Lady*, 1530(?). Oil on panel, 69.2 x 52.5 cm.

36. BEHAM, Barthel. *Portrait of Ruprecht Stüpf*, 1528. Oil on panel, 67.3 x 50.3 cm.

37. BEHAM, Barthel. *Portrait of Ursula Rudolph, Wife of Ruprecht Stüpf*, 1528. Oil on panel, 67.3 x 50.3 cm.

271.a. BEURER, Wolfgang. *Portrait of a Man*, 1487. Oil on panel, 37.3 x 27.5 cm.

244. BREU, Jörg The Elder and an anonymous artist. *Portrait of Coloman Helmschmid and Agnes Breu*, c. 1500-1505. Oil on panel, 38 x 47.9 cm.

108. CRANACH, Hans. *Hercules and the Ladies of the Court of Omphale*, 1537. Oil on panel, 57.5 x 85.3 cm.

109. CRANACH, Hans. *Portrait of a beard-*

ed Man, 1534. Oil on panel, 51.4 x 35.1 cm.

112. CRANACH, Lucas The Elder. Portrait of the Emperor Charles V, 1533. Oil on panel, 51.2 x 36 cm.

115. CRANACH. Lucas The Elder. The Nymph of the Spring, c. 1530-1534. Oil on panel, 75 x 120 cm.

113. CRANACH, Lucas The Younger. Portrait of a Woman, 1539. Oil on panel, 61.5 x 42.2 cm.

189. HOLBEIN, Hans The Elder. Portrait of a Woman, c. 1518-1520. Oil on panel, 23.6 x 17 cm.

190. HOLBEIN, Hans The Elder. Portrait of a Man, c. 1518-1520. Oil on panel, 23.7 x 17 cm.

213. MASTER OF THE MONOGRAM "TK". Portrait of a Man (Georg Thurzo?), 1518. Oil on panel, 45.5 x 33.5 cm.

214. MASTER OF THE MONOGRAM "TK". Portrait of a Woman (Anna Fugger?), 1518. Oil on panel, 44.2 x 33.2 cm.

254. MASTER OF THE LAST JUDGEMENT OF LÜNEBURG. Portrait of a young Man, c. 1485. Oil on panel, 62 x 38.5 cm.

275. MALER, Hans. Portrait of Queen Anne of Hungary and Bohemia, 1519. Oil on panel, 44 x 33.3 cm.

325. POLACK, Jan. Portrait of a Benedictine Abbot, 1484. Oil on panel, 57.3 x 41 cm.

366. SCHAFFNER, Martin. Portrait of a Man, c. 1515. Oil on panel, 35.5 x 25.5 cm.

379. STRIGEL, Bernhard. Portrait of a Man, 1528(?). Oil on panel, 42.9 x 30.3 cm.

408. TRAUT, Wolf. Portrait of a Woman, 1510. Oil on panel, 37.5 x 28.5 cm.

434. WERTINGER, Hans. Portrait of the "Knight Christopher", 1515. Oil on panel, 113 x 61.5 cm.

440. WOLGEMUT, Michael. Portrait of Levinus Memminger, c. 1485. Oil on panel, 33.7 x 22.9 cm.

443. ZEHENDER, Gabriel. Portrait of a Married Couple, 1525. Oil on panel, 40.9 x 51.5 cm.

## 16TH-CENTURY NETHERLANDISH PAINTING
## ROOM 10

9. ANONYMOUS FLEMISH around 1530. The Madonna standing, breast-feeding the Infant Christ, c. 1530. Oil on panel, 27.7 x 20.2 cm.

10. ANONYMOUS FLEMISH around 1540. The Rest on the Flight into Egypt, c. 1540. Oil on panel, 43,5 x 29.5 cm.

13. ANONYMOUS NETHERLANDISH active in Antwerp. The Madonna breast-feeding the Infant Christ, c. 1525. Watercolour and oil on cloth laid onto panel, 39.7 x 29.7 cm.

14. ANONYMOUS NETHERLANDISH from the circle of Lucas van Leyden. Saint Paul, 1525. Oil on panel, 44 x 21 cm.

34. BEER, Jan de. The Birth of the Virgin, c. 1520. Oil on panel, 111.5 x 131 cm.

35. BEER, Jan de. The Annunciation c. 1520. Oil on panel, 111.5 x 131 cm.

41. BENSON, Ambrosius. Gentleman praying, c. 1525. Oil on panel, 35.5 x 26 cm.

90. CLEVE, Joos van. The Infant Saviour standing on the World, c. 1530. Oil on panel, 37 x 26 cm.

93. COCK, Jan Wellens de. The Temptation of Saint Anthony, c. 1520. Oil on panel, 60 x 45.5 cm.

100. CORNEILLE DE LYON. Portrait of Robert de la Marck, c. 1535. Oil on panel, 18.5 x 15.5 cm.

163. GOSSAERT, Jan. Adam and Eve, c. 1507-1508. Oil on panel, 56.5 x 37 cm.

183. HEEMSKERCK, Maerten van. Portrait of a Lady spinning, c. 1531. Oil on panel, 105 x 86 cm.

220. LEYDEN, Aertgen van. Portrait of a Donor, c. 1530 (?). Oil on panel, 25.5 x 22 cm.

221. LEYDEN, Lucas Hugensz. van. The Card Players, c. 1520. Oil on panel, 29.8 x 39 cm.

249. MASTER OF FRANKFURT. The Holy Family, c. 1508. Oil on panel, 77 x 57 cm.

293. MOSTAERT, Jan. The Souls of the Just in Limbo with a Donor, c. 1520. Oil on panel, 24 x 16 cm.

294. MOSTAERT, Jan. Abraham and Hagar. Oil on panel, 94 x 131 cm.

101. OOSTSANEN, Jacob van C. Portrait of a Lady (Elizabeth of Denmark?), c. 1524. Oil on panel, 33 x 23 cm.

305. ORLEY, Bernaert van. The Rest on the Flight into Egypt, c. 1515. Oil on panel, 87 x 72 cm.

314. PATINIR, Joachim. Landscape with

the Rest on the Flight into Egypt, c. 1515-1516. Oil on panel, 31.5 x 57.5 cm.

328. PROVOST, Jan. Portrait of a female Donor, c. 1505. Oil on panel, 53.5 x 46 cm.

332. REYMERSWAELE, Marinus Claeszum van. The Calling of Saint Matthew, c. 1530. Oil on panel, 71 x 88 cm.

368. SCOREL, Jan van. The Virgin of the Daffodils with the Christ Child and two Donors, c. 1535 (?). Oil on panel, 55.5 x 76.2 cm.

414. VALCKENBORCH, Lucas van (?). The Massacre of the Innocents, 1586. Oil on panel, 76.6 x 108.1 cm.

## TITIAN, TINTORETTO, BASSANO AND EL GRECO
## ROOM 11

17. ANONYMOUS VENETIAN around 1570. The Last Supper, c. 1570. Oil on canvas, 121 x 190 cm.

31. BASSANO, Jacopo da Ponte. Pastoral Scene, c. 1560. Oil on canvas, 139 x 129 cm.

169. GRECO, El. Christ bearing the Cross, 1602-1607. Oil on canvas, 66 x 52.5 cm.

170. GRECO, El. The Immaculate Conception, 1607-1613. Oil on canvas, 108 x 82 cm.

171. GRECO, El. The Annunciation, 1596-1600. Oil on canvas, 114 x 67 cm.

172. GRECO, El. The Annunciation, 1567-1577. Oil on canvas, 117 x 98 cm.

401. TINTORETTO. The Meeting of Tamar and Judith, c. 1555-1558. Oil on canvas, 150 x 155 cm.

402. TINTORETTO. The Annunciation to the Wife of Manoah, c. 1555-1558. Oil on canvas, 150 x 155 cm.

406. TITIAN. Saint Jerome in the Desert, c. 1575. Oil on canvas, 137 x 96 cm.

## CARAVAGGIO AND THE EARLY BAROQUE
## ROOM 12

347. BABUREN, Dirck Jaspersz van (Attributed to). Saint Sebastian attended by Saint Irene and her Maid, c. 1615. Oil on canvas, 169 x 128 cm.

81. CARAVAGGIO. Saint Catherine of Alexandria, c. 1597. Oil on canvas, 173 x 133 cm.

155. GENTILESCHI, Orazio. Lot and his Daughters, c. 1621-1623. Oil on canvas, 120 x 168.5 cm.

335. RIBERA, José de. The penitent Saint Jerome, 1634. Oil on canvas, 78 x 126 cm.

336. RIBERA, José de. The Lamentation, 1633. Oil on canvas, 157 x 210 cm.

415. VALENTIN DE BOULOGNE. David with the Head of Goliath and two Soldiers, 1620-1622. Oil on canvas, 99 x 134 cm.

## 17TH-CENTURY BAROQUE PAINTING
## ROOM 13

59. BOURDON, Sébastien. The Holy Family with Saint Elizabeth and the Infant Saint John the Baptist, c. 1660-1670. Oil on canvas, 39 x 50 cm.

139. FETTI, Domenico. The Good Samaritan, 1610-1623. Oil on panel, 59.6 x 43.7 cm.

140. FETTI, Domenico. The Parable of the Sower, 1610-1623. Oil on panel, 61 x 44.5 cm.

173. GRIMALDI, Giovanni Francesco. Landscape with Tobias and the Angel, after 1650. Oil on canvas, 174 x 126 cm.

218. LE NAIN, Antoine. Children singing and playing the Violin, c. 1640. Oil on copper, 19.5 x 25.5 cm.

226. LORRAINE, Claude. Landscape with the Flight into Egypt, 1663. Oil on canvas, 193 x 147 cm.

287. MOLA, Pier Francesco. Saint John the Baptist preaching in the Desert, c. 1650-1655. Oil on canvas, 73.5 x 99 cm.

363. SALINI, Tommaso. Young Peasant Boy with a Flask, c. 1610. Oil on canvas, 99 x 73 cm.

## ROOM 14

327. PRETI, Mattia. A Concert, c. 1630-1640. Oil on canvas, 107 x 145.5 cm.

## ROOM 15

176. GUERCINO, Il. Christ and the Woman of Samaria at the Well, 1640-1641. Oil on canvas, 116 x 156 cm.

278. MARATTA, Carlo. *Saint Mark the Evangelist*, c. 1670. Oil on canvas, 101 x 74.5 cm.

296. MURILLO, Bartolomé Esteban. *The Virgin and Child with Saint Rosalina of Palermo*, c. 1670. Oil on canvas, 190 x 147 cm.

381. STROZZI, Bernardo. *Saint Cecilia*, 1623-1625. Oil on canvas, 150 x 110 cm.

448. ZURBARÁN, Francisco de. *Saint Casilda*, c. 1640-1645. Oil on canvas, 171 x 107 cm.

### 18TH-CENTURY ITALIAN PAINTING
### ROOM 16

311. PANINI, Giovanni Paolo. *The Expulsion of the Money-changers from the Temple*, 1724. Oil on canvas, 74 x 99 cm.

312. PANINI, Giovanni Paolo. *The Healing at the Pool of Bethesda*, c. 1724. Oil on canvas, 74 x 99 cm.

324. PITTONI, Giovanni Battista. *The Sacrifice of Polyxena*, 1730-1740. Oil on canvas, 72 x 58 cm.

340. RICCI, Sebastiano. *Neptune and Amphitrite*, c. 1691-1694. Oil on canvas, 94 x 75 cm.

341. RICCI, Sebastiano. *Bacchus and Ariadne*, c. 1691-1694. Oil on canvas, 94 x 75 cm.

396. TIEPOLO, Giambattista. *The Death of Sophonisba*, c. 1755-1760. Oil on canvas, 48.3 x 38.2 cm.

### ROOM 17

40. BELLOTTO, Bernardo. *Idealised View near Padua*, c. 1740-1742. Oil on canvas, 48.5 x 73 cm.

75. CANALETTO. *View of the Piazza San Marco, Venice*, before 1723. Oil on canvas, 141.5 x 204.5 cm.

76. CANALETTO. *View of the Grand Canal from San Vio, Venice*, before 1723. Oil on canvas, 140.5 x 204.5 cm.

78. CANALETTO. *The south Side of Warwick Castle*, c. 1749. Oil on canvas, 75 x 120.5 cm.

174. GUARDI, Francesco. *View of the Grand Canal with Santa Lucia and Santa Maria di Nazareth*, c. 1780. Oil on canvas, 48 x 78 cm.

175. GUARDI, Francesco. *View of the Grand Canal with San Simeone Piccolo and Santa Lucia*, c. 1780. Oil on canvas, 48 x 78 cm.

281. MARIESCHI, Michele. *View of the Grand Canal with Santa Maria della Salute*. Oil on canvas, 83.5 x 121 cm.

394. TIEPOLO, Giambattista. *The Death of Hyacinth*, 1752-1753. Oil on canvas, 287 x 235 cm.

397. TIEPOLO, Giandomenico. *The Apotheosis of Hercules*, c. 1765. Oil on canvas, 101.3 x 85.5 cm.

### ROOM 18

32. BATONI, Pompeo Girolamo. *Portrait of the contessa di San Martino*, 1785. Oil on canvas, 99 x 74 cm.

87. CERUTI, Giacomo. *Portrait of a Man*, c. 1750. Oil on canvas, 119.5 x 95.5 cm.

88. CERUTI, Giacomo. *Portrait of a Lady*, c. 1750. Oil on canvas, 119.5 x 95.5 cm.

116. CRESPI, Giuseppe Maria. *Portrait of Count Fulvio Grati*. Oil on canvas, 228 x 153 cm.

146. FOSCHI, Francesco. *Winter Landscape in the Alps*. Oil on canvas, 48 x 62 cm.

147. FOSCHI, Francesco. *Winter Landscape in the Alps.*. Oil on canvas, 48 x 62 cm.

224. LONGHI, Pietro. *The Tickle*, c. 1755. Oil on canvas, 61 x 48 cm.

316. PIAZZETTA, Giovanni Battista. *Portrait of Giulia Lama*, c. 1715. Oil on canvas, 69.4 x 55.5 cm.

337. RICCI, Marco. *Landscape with a Storm*, 1701. Oil on canvas, 89 x 146 cm.

### 17TH-CENTURY FLEMISH PAINTING
### ROOM 19

66. BRUEGHEL I, Jan. *Christ in the Storm on the Sea of Galilee*, 1596. Oil on copper, 26.6 x 35 cm.

135. DYCK, Anthony van. *Portrait of Jacques Le Roy*, 1631. Oil on canvas, 117.8 x 100.6 cm.

206. KETEL, Cornelis. *Portrait of a Gentleman aged 58*, 1594. Oil on panel, 83.2 x 65.8 cm.

207. KETEL, Cornelis. *Portrait of a Lady aged 56*, 1594. Oil on panel, 83 x 67.3 cm.

208. KEY, Adriaen Thomasz. *William I, Prince of Orange, called "William the*

*Silent"*, 1579. Oil on panel, 45.3 x 32.8 cm.

288. MASTER OF THE MONOGRAM "IDM". *View of a River Port with the Castel Sant'Angelo, Rome.* Oil on panel, 50.2 x 94 cm.

289. MASTER OF THE MONOGRAM "IDM". *View of a Village on the Banks of a River.* Oil on panel, 49.8 x 94 cm.

291. MOR, Anthonis. *Giovanni Battista di Castaldo,* c. 1550. Oil on panel, 107.6 x 82.2 cm.

350. RUBENS, Peter Paul. *Venus and Cupid,* 1606-1612. Oil on canvas, 137.2 x 111.2 cm.

351. RUBENS, Peter Paul. *The Blinding of Samson,* 1609-1610. Oil on panel, 37.5 x 58.5 cm.

352. RUBENS, Peter Paul. *Portrait of a young Woman with a Rosary,* c. 1609-1610. Oil on panel, 107 x 76.7 cm.

348. RUBENS, Peter Paul (Workshop of). *Saint Michael expelling Lucifer and the rebel Angels from Hell,* c. 1622. Oil on canvas, 149 x 126 cm.

388. TENIERS II, David and KESSEL I, Jan van. *The Surrender of the Sicilian Rebels to Antonio de Moncada in 1411,* 1663. Oil on copper, 54 x 68.2 cm.

389. TENIERS II, David and KESSEL I, Jan van. *Queen Bianca, Regent of Sicily, presenting the Captain General's Baton to Antonio de Moncada in 1410,* 1664. Oil on copper, 54.5 x 68.9 cm.

427. VOS, Cornelis de. *Antonia Canis,* 1624. Oil on copper, 123.7 x 94.2 cm.

**17TH-CENTURY DUTCH PAINTING: ITALIANATE TRENDS, AND PORTRAITS ROOM 20**

62. BREENBERGH, Bartholomeus. *Capriccio with Roman Ruins, Sculptures and a Port ,* 1650. Oil on canvas, 115.6 x 88.7 cm.

393. BRUGGHEN, Hendrick ter. *Esau selling his Birthright* c. 1627. Oil on canvas, 106,7 x 138.8 cm.

136. EVERDINGEN, Cesar van. *Vertumnus and Pomona.* Oil on panel, 47.9 x 38.9 cm.

201. JORDAENS, Jacob (and Workshop). *The Holy Family with an Angel,* c. 1618-1628. Oil on canvas, 89.7 x 103 cm.

225. LOO, Jacob van. *Group of Musicians,* c. 1650. Oil on canvas, 73.3 x 66 cm.

371. SIBERECHTS, Jan. *The Ford,* c. 1672. Oil on canvas, 63.5 x 55.4 cm.

375. STOMER, Matthias. *The Supper at Emmaus,* c. 1633-1639. Oil on canvas, 111.8 x 152.4 cm.

384. SWEERTS, Michael. *Soldiers playing Dice,* c. 1656-1658. Oil on canvas, 86.7 x 74 cm.

385. SWEERTS, Michael. *Boy in a Turban holding a Nosegay,* c. 1655. Oil on canvas, 76.4 x 61.8 cm.

442. WTEWAEL, Joachim. *The Holy Family with Saints and Angels,* c. 1606-1610. Oil on copper, 19.8 x 15.5 cm.

**ROOM 21**

51. BOL, Ferdinand. *Young Man in a feathered Cap,* c. 1647. Oil on canvas, 88.6 x 77 cm.

390. BORCH, Gerard ter. *Portrait of a Man aged 42,* 1652. Oil on copper, 24.1 x 19.3 cm.

391. BORCH, Gerard ter. *Portrait of a Woman aged 30,* c. 1652. Oil on copper, 23.9 x 18.9 cm.

392. BORCH, Gerard ter. *Portrait of a Man reading a Document,* c. 1675. Oil on canvas, 48 x 39.5 cm.

143. FLINCK, Govaert. *Portrait of a Gentleman,* 1640. Oil on panel, 67.1 x 55.1 cm.

184. HELST, Bartholomeus van der. *Portrait of a Man at a Desk with Documents,* c. 1655. Oil on canvas, 105 x 88 cm.

186. HEYDEN, Jan Jansz van der. *Corner of a Library,* c. 1710-1712. Oil on canvas, 77 x 63.5 cm.

209. KEYSER, Thomas Hendricksz de. *Portrait of two Women and a Boy,* 1632. Oil on panel, 70.2 x 50.2 cm.

242. MAES, Nicolaes. *Portrait of a Gentleman,* c. 1666-1667. Oil on canvas, 91.4 x 72.7 cm.

243. MAES, Nicolaes. *Portrait of a Lady,* 1667. Oil on canvas, 91.7 x 72.4 cm.

286. MIERIS I, Frans van. *Portrait of a Lady with a Lap-dog* 1672. Oil on panel, 31.7 x 25.4 cm.

302. NETSCHER, Caspar. *Portrait of a Lady,* 1676. Oil on canvas, 54.2 x 44.7 cm.

301. NETSCHER, Caspar (Attributed to). *Portrait of a Gentleman.* Oil on canvas, 54 x 45.4 cm.

331. REMBRANDT, Harmensz. van Rijn. *Selfportrait,* c. 1643. Oil on panel, 72 x 54.8 cm.

## 17TH-CENTURY DUTCH PAINTING: SCENES OF DAILY LIFE, INTERIORS AND LANDSCAPES ROOM 22

73. BIJLERT, Jan Hermansz van (Attributed to). *Young Man playing a Lute,* c. 1625. Oil on canvas, 97.8 x 82.6 cm.

65. BROUWER, Adriaen (Attributed to). *Village Scene with Men drinking,* c. 1631-1635. Oil on panel, 63 x 95.9 cm.

179. HALS, Frans. *Family Group in a Landscape,* c. 1645-1648. Oil on canvas, 202 x 285 cm.

178. HALS, Frans (Attributed to). *Fisherman playing the Violin,* c. 1630. Oil on canvas, 86.4 x 70 cm.

193. HONDECOETER, Melchior de. *Bird of prey in a Poultry Yard.* Oil on canvas, 122 x 139 cm.

194. HONTHORST, Gerrit van. *Merry Violinist,* c. 1624. Oil on canvas, 83 x 68 cm.

211. KONINCK, Philips Aertsz. *Panoramic Landscape with a City in the distance,* 1655. Oil on canvas, 83.4 x 127.5 cm.

## ROOM 23

154. GELDER, Aert de. *Christ and the Woman taken in Adultery,* 1683. Oil on canvas, 71.8 x 94 cm.

195. HOOCH, Pieter Hendricksz. de. *Interior with a Woman sewing and a Boy,* c. 1662-1668. Oil on canvas, 54.6 x 45.1 cm.

196. HOOCH, Pieter Hendricksz. de. *The Council Chamber of Amsterdam Town Hall,* 1661-1670. Oil on canvas, 112.5 x 99 cm.

241. MAES, Nicolaes. *The naughty Drummer,* c. 1655. Oil on canvas, 62 x 66.4 cm.

285. METSU, Gabriel. *The Cook,* c. 1657-1662. Oil on canvas, 40 x 33.7 cm.

298. NEEFFS I, Peeter. *Interior of a Church,* 1615-1616. Oil on panel, 39.3 x 58.8 cm.

306. OSTADE, Adriaen van. *Tavern Interior,* 1661. Oil on panel, 32.4 x 24.6 cm.

374. STEEN, Jan Havicksz. (Attributed to). *Country Wedding,* c. 1653. Oil on panel, 62.4 x 49.3 cm.

386. TENIERS II, David. *The Village Festival,* c. 1650. Oil on panel, 45 x 75 cm.

387. TENIERS II, David. *Smokers in an Interior,* c. 1637. Oil on panel, 39.4 x 37.3 cm.

438. WITTE, Emanuel de. *The Old Fish Market on the Dam, Amsterdam,* c. 1650. Oil on panel, 55 x 44.8 cm.

439. WITTE, Emanuel de. *Interior of a Church,* 166[9?]. Oil on panel, 52.1 x 40.2 cm.

## ROOM 24

329. BROUWER, Adriaen (Follower of). *Smoker.* Oil on panel, 19.6 x 16.1 cm.

132. DOU, Gerrit. *Young Woman with a Candle at a Window,* c. 1658-1665. Oil on panel, 26.7 x 19.5 cm.

144. FLINCK, Govaert (Attributed to). *Landscape with a Farm and a Bridge,* 1640. Oil on panel, 40.7 x 53.5 cm.

185. HEYDEN, Jan Jansz. van der. *Crossroads in a Wood.* Oil on panel, 44.5 x 55.5 cm.

222. LIEVENS, Jan. *Landscape with the Rest on the Flight into Egypt,* c.1635. Oil on panel, 34.3 x 51.8 cm.

304. OCHTERVELT, Jacob Lucasz. *Eating Oysters,* c. 1665-1669. Oil on panel, 47.6 x 37.7 cm.

307. OSTADE, Isaak van. *Traveller at a Cottage Door,* 1649. Oil on panel, 48.3 x 39.4 cm.

326. POST, Frans Jansz. *View of the Ruins of Olinfa (Recife), Brazil,* 1665. Oil on canvas, 79.8 x 111.4 cm.

365. SAVERY, Roelandt. *Mountain Landscape with a Castle,* 1609. Oil on panel, 45.6 x 63 cm.

370. SEGHERS, Hercules. *Landscape with armed Men,* c. 1625-1635. Oil on canvas, 36.5 x 54.3 cm.

373. STEEN, Jan Havicksz. *Self-portrait with Lute,* c. 1652-1665. Oil on panel, 55.3 x 43.8 cm.

419. VERMEER, Johannes. *View of Haarlem from the Dunes,* c. 1660-1670. Oil on canvas, 65.3 x 84 cm.

441. WOUWERMANS, Philips. *Horse by a River Bank,* before 1646. Oil on panel, 28.7 x 22.7 cm.

## ROOM 25

42. BERCKHEYDE, Gerrit Adriaensz. *The Nieuwezijds Voorburgwal en Amsterdam*, 1686. Oil on canvas, 53.7 x 63.9 cm.

43. BERCKHEYDE, Gerrit Adriaensz. *The Binnenhof, The Hague* c. 1690. Oil on canvas, 54.5 x 63.5 cm.

167. GOYEN, Jan Josephsz. van. *Winter Landscape with Figures on the Ice*, 1643. Oil on panel, 39.6 x 60.7 cm.

187. HOBBEMA, Meindert Lubbertsz. *Pond in a Wood*, c. 1660. Oil on canvas, 68.9 x 90.2 cm.

299. NEER, Aert van der. *Moonlight with a Path beside a Canal*, c. 1647-1650. Oil on panel, 35.6 x 65.5 cm.

300. NEER, Aert van der. *Wood with a River*, c. 1645. Oil on panel, 41.6 x 60.3 cm.

360. RUYSDAEL, Salomon Jacobsz. van. *A River with Fishermen*, 1645. Oil on panel, 51.5 x 83.6 cm.

362. SAENREDAM, Pieter Jansz. *The West Front of Saint Mary of Utrecht*, 1662. Oil on panel, 65.1 x 51.2 cm.

417. VELDE, Adriaen van de. *Pastoral Scene*, 1663. Oil on canvas, 48.5 x 62.5 cm.

437. WIJNANTS, Jan, *Castle in a Wood*, 1667. Oil on canvas, 65.3 x 52 cm.

## ROOM 26

79. CAPPELLE, Jan van de. *Seascape with Sailing Ships*, after 1652. Oil on canvas, 67.3 x 58 cm.

80. CAPPELLE, Jan van de. *Winter Landscape*, Oil on panel, 41 x 42.2 cm.

117. CUYP, Aelbert Jacobsz. *Landscape at Sunset*, after 1645. Oil on panel, 48.3 x 74.9 cm.

354. RUISDAEL, Jacob Isaacksz. van. *View of Naarden*, 1647. Oil on panel, 34.8 x 67 cm.

357. RUISDAEL, Jacob Isaacksz. van. *Path between Wheat Fields near the Zuider Zee*, c. 1660-1662. Oil on canvas, 44.8 x 54.6 cm.

358. RUISDAEL, Jacob Isaacksz. van. *View of a Canal with Commercial Buildings in Winter*, c. 1670. Oil on canvas, 65.8 x 96.7 cm.

359. RUISDAEL, Jacob Isaacksz. van. *Stormy Sea with Sailing Ships*, c. 1668. Oil on canvas, 50.1 x 62.5 cm.

355. RUISDAEL, Jacob Isaacksz. van (Attributed to). *Bleaching Fields at Bloemendael, near Haarlem*. Oil on canvas, 34.5 x 42.3 cm.

356. RUISDAEL, Jacob Isaacksz. van (Attributed to). *View inland from the coastal Dunes*, c. 1670. Oil on canvas, 52.7 x 66.7 cm.

793. RUYSDAEL, Salomon Jacobsz. van. *View of Alkmaar from the Sea*, c. 1650. Oil on panel, 36.2 x 32.5 cm.

418. VELDE II, Willem van de. *The Dutch Fleet near Goeree*, 1672-1673. Oil on canvas, 69.5 x 97.8 cm.

## 17TH-CENTURY STILL-LIFE PAINTINGS ROOM 27

1. AELST, Willem van. *Still-life with Fruit*, 1664. Oil on canvas, 67.3 x 52.1 cm.

21. AST, Balthasar van der. *Chinese Vase with Flowers*, 1628. Oil on panel, 51.6 x 33.1 cm.

56. BOSSCHAERT I, Ambrosius. *Chinese Vase with Flowers*, 1607. Oil on copper, 68.6 x 50.8 cm.

118. CHARDIN, Jean-Baptist-Siméon. *Still-life with Jug and copper Cauldron*, c. 1728-1730. Oil on canvas, 32.4 x 39.2 cm.

150. FYT, Jan. *Vase of Flowers and a Bunch of Asparagus*, c. 1650. Oil on canvas, 63.7 x 75.4 cm.

180. HAMEN Y LEON, Juan van der. *Still life-with Ceramics and Sweets*, c. 1627. Oil on canvas, 77 x 100 cm.

181. HEDA, Willem Claesz. *Still-life with a Fruit Pie and other Objects*, 1634. Oil on panel, 43.7 x 68.2 cm.

182. HEEM, Jan Davidz. de. *Glass Vase with Flowers*, c. 1665. Oil on panel, 53.4 x 41 cm.

202. KALF, Willem. *Still-life with Porcelain and a Nautilus Cup*, 1660. Oil on canvas, 64.1 x 55.9 cm.

203. KALF, Willem. *Still-life with a Chinese porcelain bowl, Nautilus Cup and other Objects*, 1662. Oil on canvas, 79.4 x 54.3 cm.

204. KALF, Willem. *Still-life with a Ewer, Fruit, Nautilus Cup and other Objects*, c. 1660. Oil on canvas, 111 x 84 cm.

223. LINARD, Jacques. *Chinese Bowl with Flowers*, 1640. Oil on canvas, 53.2 x 66 cm.

413. TRECK, Jan Jansz. (Attributed to). *Still-life with Wine Glass, pewter Jug and other Objects.* Oil on canvas, 81.8 x 57.8 cm.

376. VELDE III, Jan Jansz van de (Attributed to). *Still-life with Chinese Dish, Glass, Knife, Bread and Fruit,* c. 1650-1660. Oil on canvas, 44.7 x 38.8 cm.

## 18TH-CENTURY PAINTING: FROM ROCOCO TO NEO-CLASSICISM ROOM 28

58. BOUCHER, François. *La Toilette,* 1742. Oil on canvas, 52.5 x 66.5 cm.

119. CHARDIN, Jean-Baptist-Siméon. *Still-life with Cat and Fish ("The Lucky Thief"),* 1728. Oil on canvas, 79.5 x 63 cm.

120. CHARDIN, Jean-Baptist-Siméon. *Still-life with Cat and Rayfish ("The greedy Cat and the Oysters"),* c. 1728. Oil on canvas, 79.5 x 63 cm.

148. FRAGONARD, Jean-Honoré. *The See-Saw,* c. 1750-1755. Oil on canvas, 120 x 94.5 cm.

153. GAINSBOROUGH, Thomas. *Portrait of Sarah Buxton,* 1776-1777. Oil on canvas, 110 x 87 cm.

215. LANCRET, Nicolas. *The Swing,* c. 1735-1740. Oil on canvas, 65.5 x 54.5 cm.

216. LANCRET, Nicolas. *The Earth.* Oil on canvas, 38 x 31 cm.

217. LAWRENCE, Sir Thomas. *Portrait of David Lyon,* c. 1825. Oil on canvas, 217 x 132 cm.

219. LÉPICIÉ, Nicolas-Bernard. *In the Customs House Courtyard,* 1775. Oil on canvas, 98 x 164 cm.

279. MARÉES, Georges de. *Portrait of Maria Rosa Walburga von Soyer,* 1750. Oil on canvas, 88 x 68 cm.

280. MARÉES, Georges de. *Portrait of Franz Karl von Soyer,* 1750. Oil on canvas, 88 x 68 cm.

297. NATTIER, Jean-Marc. *Portrait of Madame Bouret as Diana,* 1745. Oil on canvas, 138 x 105 cm.

313. PATER, Jean-Baptiste-Joseph. *Concert Champêtre,* 1734. Oil on canvas, 53 x 68.5 cm.

333. REYNOLDS, Sir Joshua. *Self-portrait.* Oil on canvas, 60 x 49 cm.

334. REYNOLDS, Sir Joshua. *Portrait of Frances, Countess of Dartmouth,* 1757. Oil on canvas, 127 x 102 cm.

342. ROBERT, Hubert. *The Footbridge,* c. 1775. Oil on canvas, 59 x 47 cm.

343. ROBERT, Hubert. *Interior of the Temple of Diana, Nîmes,* 1783. Oil on canvas, 101 x 143 cm.

409. TROY, Jean-François de. *The Marriage of Jason.* Oil on canvas, 82 x 56 cm.

420. VERNET, Claude Joseph. *Stormy Sea,* 1748. Oil on canvas, 44.5 x 60.5 cm.

421. VERNET, Claude Joseph. *Calm Sea.* 1748. Oil on canvas, 44.5 x 60.5 cm.

431. WATTEAU, Jean Antoine. *The Rest,* c. 1709. Oil on canvas, 32 x 42.5 cm.

432. WATTEAU, Jean Antoine. *Pierrot Content,* c. 1712. Oil on canvas, 35 x 31 cm.

444. ZOFFANY, Johann. *Portrait of Ann Brown in the Role of Miranda,* c. 1770. Oil on canvas, 218 x 158.5 cm.

445. ZOFFANY, Johann. *Group Portrait with Sir Elijah and Lady Impey,* 1783-1784. Oil on canvas, 91.5 x 122 cm.

## 19TH-CENTURY NORTH AMERICAN PAINTING ROOM 29

468. BIERSTADT, Albert. *Dusk on the Prairie,* c. 1870. Oil on canvas, 81.3 x 123 cm.

508. CHURCH, Frederic Edwin. *Cross in a remote Landscape,* 1859. Oil on canvas, 41.3 x 61.5 cm.

509. CHURCH, Frederic Edwin. *Abandoned Rowing Boat,* 1850. Oil on cardboard, 28 x 43.2 cm.

91. CLONNEY, James Goodwyn. *Fishing Party on Long Island Sound off New Rochelle,* 1847. Oil on canvas, 66 x 92.7 cm.

95. COLE, Thomas. *Expulsion. Moon and Firelight,* c. 1828. Oil on canvas, 91.4 x 122 cm.

96. COLE, Thomas. *Cross at Sunset.* c. 1848. Oil on canvas, 81.3 x 123.2 cm.

97. COPLEY, John Singleton. *Portrait of Catherine Hill, Wife of Joshua Henshaw II,* c. 1772. Oil on canvas, 77 x 56 cm.

98. COPLEY, John Singleton. *Portrait of Miriam Kilby, Wife of Samuel Hill,* c. 1764. Oil on canvas, 128.4 x 102 cm.

99. COPLEY, John Singleton. *Portrait of Judge Martin Howard,* 1767. Oil on canvas, 125.7 x 101 cm.

533. DURAND, Asher Brown. *A Creek in the Wood*, 1865. Oil on canvas, 101.6 x 81.9 cm.

577. HEADE, Martin Johnson. *Singing Beach, Manchester*, 1862. Oil on canvas, 63.5 x 127 cm.

601. INNESS, George. *Summer Days*, 1857. Oil on canvas, 103.5 x 143 cm.

612. KENSETT, John Frederick. *Lake George*, c. 1860. Oil on canvas, 55.8 x 86.4 cm.

633. LANE, Fitz Hugh. *The Fort and Ten Pound Island, Gloucester, Massachusetts*, 1847. Oil on canvas, 50.8 x 76.2 cm.

315. PEALE, Charles Wilson. *Portrait of Isabella and John Stewart*, c. 1775. Oil on canvas, 94 x 124 cm.

701. PETO, John Frederick. *Sailing at Dusk*, c. 1890. Oil on canvas, 30.5 x 50.9 cm.

722. REMINGTON, Frederic. *Apache Fire Signal* c, 1908. Oil on canvas, 102 x 68.5 cm.

364. SALMON, Robert. *Greenock, Scotland*, 1816. Oil on canvas, 66.6 x 112.3 cm.

760. SILVA, Francis A. *Kingston Point on the Hudson River*, c. 1873. Oil on canvas, 51 x 91 cm.

383. STUART, Gilbert. *Supposed Portrait of George Washington's Cook*, Oil on canvas, 76 x 63.5 cm.

## ROOM 30

501. CHASE, William Merritt. *The Kimono*, c. 1895. Oil on canvas, 89. 5 x 115 cm.

502. CHASE, William Merritt. *Shinnecock Hills*, 1893-1897. Oil on panel, 44.4 x 54.6 cm.

507. CHURCH, Frederic Edwin. *Autumn*, 1875. Oil on canvas, 39.4 x 61 cm.

496. CROPSEY, Jasper Francis. *Lake Greenwood*, 1870. Oil on canvas, 97 x 174 cm.

574. HARNETT, William M. *Materials for a Leisure Hour*, 1879. Oil on canvas, 38 x 51.5 cm.

588. HOMER, Winslow. *The Distress Signal*, 1890. Oil on canvas, 62 x 98 cm.

589. HOMER, Winslow. *Waverly Oaks*, 1864. Oil on paper laid down on panel, 33.6 x 25.4 cm.

591. HOMER, Winslow. *Portrait of Helena de Kay*, c. 1873. Oil on panel, 31 x 47 cm.

600. INNESS, George. *Morning*, c. 1878. Oil on canvas, 76.2 x 114.3 cm.

646. LEWIS, Henry. *The Falls of Saint Anthony, Upper Mississippi*, 1847. Oil on canvas, 68.6 x 82.5 cm.

700. PETO, John Frederick. *"Tom's River"*, 1905. Oil on canvas, 50.8 x 40.6 cm.

702. PETO, John Frederick. *Books, Mug, Pipe and Violin*, c. 1880. Oil on canvas, 63.5 x 50.9 cm.

725. ROBINSON, Theodore. *The Old Bridge*, 1890. Oil on canvas, 63.5 x 81.2 cm.

731. SARGENT, John Singer. *Venetian Onion-seller*, 1882. Oil on canvas, 95 x 70 cm.

732. SARGENT, John Singer. *Portrait of Millicent, Duchess of Sutherland*, 1904. Oil on canvas, 254 x 146 cm.

761. SLOAN, John. *Throbbing Fountain in Madison Square*, 1907. Oil on canvas, 66 x 81.5 cm.

784. WHISTLER, James Abbott McNeill. *Rose and gold: the Neapolitan*, c. 1897. Oil on canvas, 50 x 31 cm.

785. WIMAR, Carl. *The lost Trail*, c. 1856. Oil on canvas, 49.5 x 77.5 cm.

## 19TH-CENTURY EUROPEAN PAINTING: FROM ROMANTICISM TO REALISM
## ROOM 31

494. COROT, Jean-Baptiste-Camille. *Setting out for a Walk in the Parc des Lions, Port-Marly*, c. 1872. Oil on canvas, 78 x 65 cm.

493. COROT, Jean-Baptiste-Camille. *Interior of the Church at Mantes*, 1865-1870. Oil on canvas, 35 x 22.5 cm.

495. COURBET, Gustave. *The Stream at Brème*, 1866. Oil on canvas, 114 x 89 cm.

126. DELACROIX, Eugène. *Arab Rider*, c.1854. Oil on canvas, 35 x 26.5 cm.

127. DELACROIX, Eugène. *The Duke of Orléans revealing his Lover*, c. 1825-1826. Oil on canvas, 35 x 25.5 cm.

541. FANTIN-LATOUR, Henri. *Vase of Chrysanthemums*, 1875. Oil on canvas, 42.5 x 39.5 cm.

792. FRIEDRICH, Caspar David. *Easter Morning*, 1833. Oil on canvas, 43.7 x 34.4 cm.

157. GERICAULT, Théodore. *A Scene from the free Horse Race*, 1816-1817. Oil on paper laid down on canvas, 44 x 59 cm.

164. GOYA Y LUCIENTES, Francisco José de. *King Ferdinand VII of Spain*, 1814-1815. Oil on canvas, 84 x 63.5 cm.

165. GOYA Y LUCIENTES, Francisco José de. *El Tío Paquete*, c. 1819-1820. Oil on canvas, 39 x 31 cm.

166. GOYA Y LUCIENTES, Francisco José de. *Asensio Julià*, c. 1798. Oil on canvas, 54.5 x 41 cm.

177. HACKERT, Jacob-Philipp. *Landscape with the Palace of Caserta and Vesuvius*, 1793. Oil on canvas, 93 x 130 cm.

604. JONGKIND, Johann Barthold. *View of the Port of Rotterdam*, 1856. Oil on canvas, 43 x 56 cm.

205. KAUFFMANN, Angelica. *Portrait of a Lady as a Vestal Virgin*, Oil on canvas, 60 x 41 cm.

292. MORGENSTERN, Christian. *Trees at the Water's Edge*, 1832. Oil on canvas, 71 x 100.5 cm.

775. TRUEBNER, Wilhelm. *Flowerpiece*, Oil on canvas, 30 x 22.5 cm.

## IMPRESSIONIST AND POST-IMPRESSIONIST PAINTING
## ROOM 32

476. BOUDIN, Eugène. *The Square with the Church of Saint Vulfran, Abbeville*, 1884. Oil on panel, 44.5 x 37 cm.

552. GAUGUIN, Paul. *Man on the Road (Rouen)*, 1884. Oil on canvas, 73 x 92 cm.

659. MANET, Edouard. *Woman in a Riding Habit, full-face*, c. 1882. Oil on canvas, 73 x 52 cm.

680. MONET, Claude. *The Thaw at Vétheuil*, 1881. Oil on canvas, 60 x 100 cm.

686. MORISOT, Berthe. *The Dressing Mirror*, 1876. Oil on canvas, 65 x 54 cm.

711. PISSARRO, Camille. *The Wood at Marly*, 1871. Oil on canvas, 45 x 55 cm.

712. PISSARRO, Camille. *Afternoon on the rue Saint-Honoré. Effect of Rain*, 1897. Oil on canvas, 81 x 65 cm.

724. RENOIR, Pierre-Auguste. *Woman with a Parasol in a Garden*, c. 1873. Oil on canvas, 54.5 x 65 cm.

779. VUILLARD, Edouard. *The Singer*, 1891-1892. Pastel on paper, 28 x 20 cm.

## ROOM 33

473. BONNARD, Pierre. *Portrait of Misia Godebska*, 1908. Oil on canvas, 145 x 114 cm.

488. CEZANNE, Paul. *Portrait of a Peasant*, 1901-1906, Oil on canvas, 65 x 54 cm.

515. DEGAS, Edgar. *Swaying Dancer (Green Dancer)*, 1877-1879. Pastel on paper, 66 x 36 cm.

516. DEGAS, Edgar. *At the Milliner's*, c. 1883. Pastel on paper, 75.9 x 84.8 cm.

557. GOGH, Vincent van. *Stevedores in Arles*, 1888. Oil on canvas, 54 x 65 cm.

559. GOGH, Vincent van. *"Les Vessenots", Auvers*, 1890. Oil on canvas, 55 x 65 cm.

788. GOGH, Vincent van. *Landscape at Dusk*, 1885. Oil on canvas mounted on cardboard, 35 x 43 cm.

773. TOULOUSE-LAUTREC, Henri de. *Gaston Bonnefoy*, 1891. Oil on cardboard, 71 x 37 cm.

774. TOULOUSE-LAUTREC, Henri de. *The Red-head in a white Blouse*, 1889. Oil on canvas, 59.5 x 48.2 cm.

## FAUVE PAINTING
## ROOM 34

524. DERAIN, André. *Waterloo Bridge*, 1906. Oil on canvas, 80.5 x 101 cm.

759. SICKERT, Walter Richard. *Giuseppina la Bague*, 1903-1904. Oil on canvas, 45.7 x 38.2 cm.

## EXPRESSIONIST PAINTING
## ROOM 35

534. ENSOR, James. *The Theatre of Masks*, 1908. Oil on canvas, 72 x 86 cm.

629. KOKOSCHKA, Oskar. *Portrait of Max Schmidt*, 1914. Oil on canvas, 90 x 57.5 cm.

664. MATISSE, Henri. *Yellow Flowers*, 1902. Oil on canvas, 46 x 54.5 cm.

689. MUNCH, Edvard. *Dusk. Laura, the Artist's Sister*, 1888. Oil on canvas, 75 x 100.5 cm.

739. SCHIELE, Egon. *Houses next to the River. The Old City*, 1914. Oil on canvas, 100 x 120.5 cm.

## ROOM 36

579. HECKEL, Erich. *The Brick Factory. Dangast*, 1907. Oil on canvas, 68 x 86 cm.

693. NOLDE, Emil. *The Garden Path*, 1906. Oil on canvas, 52.4 x 55.8 cm.

742. SCHMIDT-ROTTLUFF, Karl. *Autumn Landscape, Oldenburg*, 1907. Oil on canvas, 76 x 97.5 cm

## ROOM 37

613. KIRCHNER, Ernst Ludwig. *Doris in a high Collar*, c. 1906. Oil on cardboard, 70.5 x 51 cm.

789. KIRCHNER, Ernst Ludwig. *Fränzi in front of a carved Chair*, 1910. Oil on canvas, 71 x 49.5 cm.

615.a. KIRCHNER, Ernst Ludwig. *Nude kneeling before a red Screen*, 1912. Oil on canvas, 75 x 56 cm.

615.b. KIRCHNER, Ernst Ludwig. *Seated Nude. Study*, 1912. Oil on canvas, 75 x 56 cm.

616. KIRCHNER, Ernst Ludwig. *Alpine Kitchen*, 1918. Oil on canvas, 121.5 x 121.5 cm.

618. KIRCHNER, Ernst Ludwig. *The Bay*, c. 1914. Oil on canvas, 146 x 123 cm.

687. MUELLER, Otto. *Female Nudes in a Landscape*, c. 1922. Oil on hessian, 100 x 138 cm.

690. NOLDE, Emil. *Autumn. Dusk*, 1924. Oil on canvas, 73 x 100.5 cm.

691. NOLDE, Emil. *Summer Clouds*, 1913. Oil on canvas, 73.3 x 88.5 cm.

692. NOLDE, Emil. *Sunflowers*, 1936. Oil on canvas, 88.5 x 67.3 cm.

699. PECHSTEIN, Max. *Summer in Nidden*, 1919-1920. Oil on canvas, 81.3 x 101 cm.

## ROOM 38

485. BURLIUK, David. *Landscape*, 1912. Oil on canvas, 33 x 46.3 cm.

543. FEININGER, Lyonel. *Lady in Mauve*, 1922, Oil on canvas, 100.5 x 80.5 cm.

544. FEININGER, Lyonel. *Ships*, 1917. Oil on canvas, 71 x 85.5 cm.

545. FEININGER, Lyonel. *Architecture II (The Man from Potin)*, 1921. Oil on canvas, 101 x 80.5 cm.

602. ITTEN, Johannes. *Group of Houses in Spring*, 1916. Oil on canvas, 90 x 75 cm.

603. JAWLENSKY, Alexej von. *The red Veil*, 1912. Oil on cardboard, 64.5 x 54 cm.

611. KANDINSKY, Wassily. *Johannisstrasse, Murnau*, 1908. Oil on cardboard, 70 x 48.5 cm.

655. MACKE, August. *Galloping Hussars*, 1913. Oil on canvas, 37.5 x 56.1 cm.

656. MACKE, August. *Circus*, 1913. Oil on cardboard, 47 x 63.5 cm.

660. MARC, Franz. *The Dream*, 1912. Oil on canvas, 100.5 x 135.5 cm.

## ROOM 39

463. BECKMANN, Max. *Still-life with yellow Roses*, 1937, Oil on canvas, 110.5 x 65.5 cm.

464. BECKMANN, Max. *Quappi in a pink Sweater*, 1935. Oil on canvas, 105 x 73 cm.

465. BECKMANN, Max. *Self-portrait with Hand raised*, 1908. Oil on canvas, 55 x 45 cm.

637. LARIONOV, Michail. *The Baker*, 1909. Oil on canvas, 107 x 102 cm.

638. LARIONOV, Michail. *Blue Nude*, 1903. Oil on canvas, 73 x 116 cm.

## ROOM 40

525. DIX, Otto. *Hugo Erfurth with a Dog*, 1926. Tempera and oil on panel, 80 x 100 cm.

569. GROSZ, George. *Metropolis*, 1916-1917. Oil on canvas, 100 x 102 cm.

572. GROSZ, George. *Street Scene (Kurfürstendamm)*, 1925. Oil on canvas, 81.3 x 61.3 cm.

582. HENRICH, Albert. *Portrait of the Painter A. M. Tränkler*. Oil on canvas, 81 x 62 cm.

596. HUBBUCH, Karl. *Double Portrait of Hilde II*, c. 1929. Oil on canvas mounted on board, 150 x 77 cm.

614. KIRCHNER, Ernst Ludwig. *Berlin Street Scene*, 1914-1925. Oil on canvas, 125 x 90.5 cm.

671. MEIDNER, Ludwig. *The House on the Corner (The Villa Kochmann in Dres-*

den), 1913. Oil on canvas mounted on board, 97.2 x 78 cm.

733. SCHAD, Christian. *Portrait of Doctor Haustein*, 1928. Oil on canvas, 80.5 x 55 cm.

734. SCHAD, Christian. *Maria and Annunziata from the Port*, 1923. Oil on canvas, 67.5 x 55.5 cm.

741. SCHLICHTER, Rudolf. *Portrait of an Oriental Journalist*, c. 1924. Oil on canvas, 73.5 x 50.5 cm.

## THE EXPERIMENTAL AVANT-GARDES
## ROOM 41

459. BALLA, Giacomo. *Patriotic Demonstration*, 1915. Oil on canvas, 100 x 136.5 cm.

478. BRAQUE, Georges. *Woman with a Mandolin*, 1910. Oil on canvas, 80.5 x 54 cm.

517. DELAUNAY, Robert. *Woman with a Parasol. The Parisian*, 1913. Oil on canvas, 122 x 85.5 cm.

518. DELAUNAY-TERK, Sonia. *Simultaneous Contrasts*, 1913. Oil on canvas, 55 x 46 cm.

519. DELAUNAY-TERK, Sonia. *Simultaneous Dresses (The three Women)* , 1925. Oil on canvas, 146 x 114 cm.

555. GLEIZES, Albert. *In the Port (Looking at the Port)*, 1917. Oil and sand on board, 153 x 120 cm.

562. GONTCHAROVA, Natalia. *Rayonist Landscape. The Wood*, 1913. Oil on canvas, 130 x 97 cm.

567. GRIS, Juan. *The Smoker*, 1913. Oil on canvas, 73 x 54 cm.

634. KUPKA, Frantisek. *Positioning of Mobile Graphic Elements I*, 1912-1913. Oil on canvas, 200 x 194 cm.

790. KUPKA, Frantisek. *Study for the Language of Verticals*, 1911. Oil on canvas, 78 x 63 cm.

645. LÉGER, Fernand. *The Staircase (Second State)*, 1914. Oil on canvas, 88 x 124.5 cm.

678. MONDRIAN, Piet. *Composition in grey-blue*, 1912-1913. Oil on canvas, 79.5 x 63.5 cm.

707. PICASSO, Pablo Ruiz. *Head of a Man*, 1913-1914. Oil on canvas, 65 x 46 cm.

710. PICASSO, Pablo Ruiz. *Man with a Clarinet*, 1911-1912. Oil on canvas, 106 x 69 cm.

715. POPOVA, Liubov. *Still-life with Instruments*, 1915. Oil on canvas, 105.5 x 69.2 cm.

752. SEVERINI, Gino. *Expansion of Light*, 1912. Oil on canvas, 68.5 x 43.2 cm.

## ROOM 42

526. DOESBURG, Theo van. *Pictorial Motif. Still-life*, 1916. Oil on canvas, 45 x 32 cm.

633. KUPKA, Frantisek. *The Drill*, 1925. Oil on canvas, 73 x 85 cm.

730. ROZANOVA, Olga. *Man in the Street (Analysis of Volumes)*, 1913. Oil on canvas, 83 x 61.5 cm.

776. UDALZOVA, Nadeshda. *Cubism*, 1914. Oil on canvas, 72 x 60 cm.

780. WADSWORTH, Edward. *Vorticist Composition*, 1915. Oil on canvas, 76.3 x 63.5 cm.

## ROOM 43

481. BRUCE, Patrick Henry. *Painting. Still-life*, c. 1923-1924. Oil and pencil on canvas, 63.5 x 81.3 cm.

506. CHASHNIK, Ilya. *Suprematist Composition*, 1923. Oil on canvas, 183.5 x 112 cm.

528. DOESBURG, Theo van. *Composition XX*, 1919-1920. Oil on canvas, 92 x 71 cm.

625. KLIUN, Ivan Wasilewitsch. *Composition*, 1917. Oil on canvas, 88 x 69 cm.

641. LECK, Bart van der. *Mountain Landscape in Algeria with a Village*, 1917. Gouache on fibrous paper, 100 x 154 cm.

642. LECK, Bart van der. *Woodcutter*, 1927. Oil on canvas, 59 x 70.5 cm.

651. LISSITZKY, Eliezer. *Proun 4 B*, 1919-1920. Oil on canvas, 70 x 55.5 cm.

652. LISSITZKY, Eliezer. *Proun 1 C*, 1919. Oil on cardboard, 68 x 68 cm.

675. MOHOLY-NAGY, László. *Large Railway Painting*, 1920. Oil on canvas, 100 x 77 cm.

676. MOHOLY-NAGY, László. *Circle Segments*, 1921. Tempera on canvas, 78 x 60 cm.

677. MONDRIAN. Piet, *Colour Composition I.* 1931, Oil on canvas, 50 x 50 cm.

679, MONDRIAN, Piet. *New York City, New York*, 1940-1942. Oil, pencil, charcoal and tape on canvas, 117 x 110 cm.

714. POPOVA, Liubov. *Painterly Architectonic*, 1918. Oil on canvas, 45 x 53 cm.

716. POPOVA, Liubov. *Architectonic Composition*, c. 1917. Oil on hessian, 70.5 x 70.5 cm.

745. SCHWITTERS, Kurt. *Eight-sided Composition*, 1930. Oil on board, 91 x 90 cm.

767. SUETIN, Nikolai. *Suprematism*, 1920-1921. Oil on canvas, 53 x 70.5 cm.

778. VORDEMBERGE-GILDEWART, Friedrich. *Composition nº 104. White on white*, 1936. Oil on canvas, 60 x 60 cm.

782. WEBER, Max. *Grand Central Station*, 1915. Oil on canvas, 152.5 x 101.6 cm.

**ROOM 44**

453. ANNENKOV, Yuri. *Amiens Cathedral*, 1919, Collage, wood, cardboard and wire on paper, 71 x 52 cm.

536. ERNST, Max. *Flower-Shell*, 1927. Oil on canvas, 19 x 24 cm.

538. ERNST, Max. *Untitled. (Dada)*, c. 1922. Oil on canvas, 43.2 x 31.5 cm.

546. FILONOV, Pavel Nikolaevitch and GLEBOVA, Tatiana. *MOPR. Prison*, 1927. Oil on canvas, 236.5 x 153 cm.

735. SCHAD, Christian. *Composition in N*, 1919. Box with wood and collage relief on hessian, 18 x 25 x 2.2 cm.

746. SCHWITTERS, Kurt. *Merzbild 1A (The Psychiatrist)*, 1919. Mixed technique and montage on canvas, 48.5 x 38.5 cm.

747. SCHWITTERS, Kurt. *Merzbild Kijkduin*, 1923. Mixed media on cardboard, 74.3 x 60.3 cm.

748. SCHWITTERS, Kurt. *Merz 1925, 1. Relief in a blue Square*, 1925. Mixed media on cardboard, 49.5 x 50.2 cm.

**THE SYNTHESIS OF MODERNITY IN EUROPE AND THE UNITED STATES ROOM 45**

461. BAUMEISTER, Willi. *Black Ghost*, 1952. Oil and sand on cardboard, 81 x 100 cm.

480. BRAQUE, Georges. *The pink Tablecloth*, 1938. Oil and sand on canvas, 87.5 x 106 cm.

497. CHAGALL, Marc. *The Madonna of the Village*, 1938-1942. Oil on canvas, 102.5 x 98 cm.

499. CHAGALL, Marc. *The Rooster*, 1928. Oil on canvas, 81 x 65.5 cm.

500. CHAGALL, Marc. *The grey House*, 1917. Oil on canvas, 68 x 74 cm.

537. ERNST, Max. *33 Girls in search of the white Butterfly*, 1958. Oil on canvas, 137 x 107 cm.

566. GRIS, Juan. *Bottle and Fruit Dish*, 1919. Oil on canvas, 74 x 54 cm.

606. KANDINSKY, Wassily. *Around the Line*, 1943. Oil on cardboard, 42 x 57.8 cm.

608. KANDINSKY, Wassily. *In the bright Oval*, 1925. Oil on cardboard, 73 x 59 cm.

609. KANDINSKY, Wassily. *Painting with three Spots. Nº 196*, 1914. Oil on canvas, 121 x 111 cm.

622. KLEE, Paul. *View of a Square*, 1912. Mixed media on paper, 16.5 x 27 cm (visible surface).

623. KLEE, Paul. *Omega 5. (Dummy)*, 1927. Oil and watercolour on canvas stuck to cardboard, 57.3 x 43 cm.

624. KLEE, Paul. *Revolving House*, 1921. Gouache on cheesecloth stuck to paper, 37.7 x 52.2 cm.

643. LÉGER, Fernand. *Composition. The Disk*, 1918. Oil on canvas, 65 x 54 cm.

672. MIRÓ, Joan. *Catalan Peasant with Guitar*, 1924. Oil on canvas, 147 x 114 cm.

673. MIRÓ, Joan. *White-ground Painting*, 1927. Oil on canvas, 55 x 46 cm.

706. PICASSO, Pablo Ruiz. *Bull-fight*, 1934. Oil on canvas, 54 x 73 cm.

709. PICASSO, Pablo Ruiz. *Harlequin with a Mirror*, 1923. Oil on canvas, 100 x 81 cm.

764. STAEL, Nicolas de. *Grey Composition*, 1948. Oil on canvas, 150 x 75 cm.

**ROOM 46**

563. GORKY, Arshile. *Hugging / (Good Hope Road II) / (Pastoral)*, 1945. Oil on canvas, 64.7 x 82.7 cm.

564. GORKY, Arshile. *Last Painting (The Black Monk)*, 1948 Oil on canvas, 78.6 x 101.5 cm.

587. HOFMANN, Hans. *Untitled (Renate Series)*, 1965. Oil on canvas, 121.9 x 91.4 cm.

630. KOONING, Willem de. *Abstraction*, 1949-1950. Mixed media on plywood cardboard, 37 x 46.5 cm.

631. KOONING, Willem de. *Red Man with Moustache*, 1971. Oil on paper mounted on canvas, 186 x 91.5 cm.

653. LOUIS, Morris. *The Columns of Hercules*, 1960. Acrylic on canvas, 231.1 x 267.3 cm.

670. MATTA, Roberto Sebastian Antonio. *Untitled*, 1942-1943. Oil on canvas, 30.5 x 40.5 cm.

674. MIRÓ, Joan. *The Lightning Bird blinded by the Fire of the Moon*, 1955. Oil on cardboard, 26 x 20 cm.

695. O'KEEFFE, Georgia. *Abstraction*, 1920. Oil on canvas, 71 x 61 cm.

697. O'KEEFFE, Georgia. *White Iris nº 7*, 1957. Oil on canvas, 76.2 x 102 cm.

713. POLLOCK, Jackson. *Brown and Silver I*, c. 1951. Enamel and silver paint on canvas, 145 x 101 cm.

729. ROTHKO, Mark. *Green on Maroon*, 1961. Mixed media on canvas, 258 x 229 cm.

766. STILL, Clyfford. *Untitled*, 1965. Oil on canvas, 254 x 176.5 cm.

771. TOBEY, Mark. *Earth Rhythms*, 1961. Gouache on cardboard, 67 x 49 cm.

## LATE SURREALISM, THE FIGURATIVE TRADITION AND POP ART
## ROOM 47

455. AUERBACH, Frank. *Head of J.Y.M.*, 1978. Oil on canvas, 61 x 66 cm.

460. BALTHUS (Balthasar Klossowsky de ROLA). *The Card Game*, 1948-1950. Oil on canvas, 140 x 194 cm.

491. CORNELL, Joseph. *Cockatoo Juan Gris Nº 4*, c. 1953-1954. Construction, 50 x 30 x 11.5 cm.

492. CORNELL, Joseph. *Blue Soap Bubble*, 1949-1950. Construction, 24.5 x 30.5 x 9.6 cm.

510. DALÍ, Salvador. *Dream caused by the Flight of a Bee around a Pomegranate one Second before Awakening*, 1944. Oil on cardboard, 51 x 41 cm.

511. DALÍ, Salvador. *Gradiva finds the Ruins of Anthropomorphos*, 1931-1932. Oil on canvas, 65 x 54 cm.

513. DAVIS, Stuart. *Sweet Caporal*, 1922. Oil and watercolour on canvas-covered cardboard, 51 x 47 cm.

520. DELVAUX, Paul. *Woman before a Mirror*, 1936. Oil on canvas, 71 x 91.5 cm.

535. ERNST, Max. *Single and conjugal Trees*, 1942. Oil on canvas, 81.5 x 100.5 cm.

554. GIACOMETTI,, Alberto. *Portrait of a Woman*, 1965. Oil on canvas, 86 x 65 cm.

556. GNOLI, Domenico. *Armchair*, 1967. Oil and sand on cardboard, 200 x 140. 5 cm.

594. HOPPER, Edward. *Hotel Room*, 1931. Oil on canvas, 152.4 x 165.7 cm.

595. HOPPER, Edward. *Girl at a Sewing Machine*, 1921-1922. Oil on canvas, 48.3 x 46 cm.

632. KOSSOFF, Leon. *Ticket Hall. Kilburn Underground Station No. 1*, 1976. Oil on cardboard, 45.7 x 38.1 cm.

657. MAGRITTE, René. *The Key of the Field*, 1936. Oil on canvas, 80 x 60 cm.

754. SHAHN, Ben. *Four-piece Orchestra*, 1944. Tempera on masonite, 45.7 x 60.1 cm.

756. SHAHN, Ben. *Carnival*, 1946. Tempera on masonite, 56 x 75.5 cm.

768. TANGUY, Yves. *Imaginary Numbers*, 1954. Oil on canvas, 99 x 80 cm.

769. TANGUY, Yves. *Composition (Death watching his Family)*, 1927. Oil on canvas, 100 x 73 cm.

770. TANGUY, Yves. *Still and Always*, 1942. Oil on canvas, 100 x 81 cm.

787. WYETH, Andrew. *My young Friend*, 1970. Tempera on masonite, 81.3 x 63.5 cm.

## ROOM 48

452. ANDREWS, Michael. *Lights V. The Pier Pavilion*, 1973. Acrylic on canvas, 152.4 x 213.3 cm.

458. BACON, Francis. *Portrait of George Dyer in a Mirror*, 1968. Oil on canvas, 198 x 147 cm.

514. DAVIS, Stuart. *Pochade*, 1958. Oil on canvas, 130 x 152 cm.

548. FREUD, Lucian. *Last Portrait*, 1976-1977. Oil on canvas, 61 x 61 cm.

549. FREUD, Lucian. *Large Interior. Paddington*, 1968-1969. Oil on canvas, 183 x 122 cm.

550. FREUD, Lucian. *Reflection with two Children (Self-portrait)*, 1965. Oil on canvas, 91 x 91 cm.

551. FREUD, Lucian. *Portrait of Baron H. H. Thyssen-Bornemisza*, 1981-1982. Oil on canvas, 51 x 40 cm.

584. HOCKNEY, David. *In Memory of Cecchino Bracci*, 1962. Oil on canvas, 213.3 x 91.4 cm.

619. KITAJ, Ronald B. *The Greek from Smyrna (Nicos)*, 1976-1977. Oil on canvas, 243.8 x 76.2 cm.

620. KITAJ, Ronald B. *A Visit to London (Robert Creeley and Robert Duncan)*, 1977. Oil on canvas, 182.9 x 61 cm.

648. LICHTENSTEIN, Roy. *Woman in the Bath*, 1963. Oil on canvas, 171 x 171 cm.

649. LINDNER, Richard. *Moon over Alabama*, 1963. Oil on canvas, 202 x 102 cm.

721. RAUSCHENBERG, Robert. *Express*, 1963. Oil on canvas with screenprint, 183 x 305 cm.

728. ROSENQUIST, James. *Smoked Glass*, 1962. Oil on canvas, 61 x 81.5 cm.

783. WESSELMANN, Tom. *Nude No. 1*, 1970. Oil on canvas, 63.5 x 114.5 cm.

## STAIRS

486. BURLIUK, Vladimir. *Russian Peasant Woman*, 1910-1911. Oil on canvas, 132 x 70 cm.

490. CORINTH, Lovis. *Fashion Show*, 1921. Oil on canvas, 201.5 x 100 cm.

523. DEPERO, Fortunato. *Robot with Pipe*, 1920. Gouache on paper mounted on canvas, 67.5 x 52.5 cm.

129. DOLCI, Carlo. *The Christ Child with a Crown of Flowers*, 1663. Oil on canvas, 103 x 71 cm.

138. FENZONI, Ferrau. *Saint Francis receiving the Stigmata*. Oil on canvas, 108 x 82 cm.

160. GHIRLANDI, Fra Vittore. *Portrait of a Goldsmith*. Oil on canvas, 73 x 57 cm.

617. KIRCHNER, Ernst Ludwig. *The Junker-boden under Snow*. Oil on canvas, 100 x 120 cm.

688. MUENTER, Gabriele. *Self-portrait*, c. 1908. Oil on cardboard, 49 x 33.6 cm.

367. SCHOENFELD, Heinrich. *Solomon and the Queen of Sheba*. Oil on canvas, 82 x 112 cm.

338. RICCI, Marco. *Winter Landscape*. Oil on canvas, 173 x 232 cm.

## PATIO

765. STELLA, Frank. *Untitled*, 1966. Alkyd on canvas, 91.5 x 91.5 cm.

539. ESTES, Richard. *Telephone Booths*, 1967. Acrylic on masonite, 122 x 175.3 cm.

547. FONTANA, Lucio. *Venice was all gold*, 1961. Acrylic on canvas, 149 x 149 cm.

## CAFETERIA AND AUDITORIUM AREA

573. GUTTUSO, Renato. *Café Greco*, 1976. Acrylic on canvas-covered cardboard, 186 x 243 cm.

665. MATTA, Roberto Sebastian Antonio. *Great Expectations*. From the cycle: "The blinding Exile", 1966. Oil on canvas, 203 x 402 cm.

666. MATTA, Roberto Sebastian Antonio. *Where Madness dwells A*. From the cycle: "The blinding Exile", 1966. Oil on canvas, 205 x 203.5 cm.

667. MATTA, Roberto Sebastian Antonio. *The blinding Exile*. From the cycle: "The blinding Exile", 1966. Oil on canvas, 200 x 195 cm.

668. MATTA, Roberto Sebastian Antonio. *The Where at High Tide*. From the cycle: "The blinding Exile", 1966. Oil on canvas, 202 x 195 cm.

669. MATTA, Roberto Sebastian Antonio. *Where Madness dwells B*. From the cycle: "The blinding Exile", 1966. Oil on canvas, 204 x 204.5 cm.

Publishing coordinator: *Laura Estévez*
Layout: *Maite Caffaratto*
Photographs:
*José Loren*
*Joaquín Cortés*
*Villa Favorita*
Translated by
*Laura A. E. Suffield*